HOW TO DISSOLVE UNWANTED EMOTIONS

BECOMING HAPPIER

DENNIS E. BRADFORD, PH.D.

Legalities

By The Same Author

To

Joyce and Beatrice

Preface

This is primarily a how-to manual. If you're in emotional distress and reading it because you want to learn how to alleviate and eliminate that distress, please go directly to Chapter 5 to understand the skill (technique, method) that will enable you to do that.

There will, of course, be some points made there that you won't understand because you haven't read the previous four chapters, but don't worry about that. Reading them is not necessary to make use the valuable skill taught in Chapter 5. After you've begun to enjoy greater freedom from unwanted emotions, I strongly encourage you to go back and read the book from beginning to end.

Why? It's because doing so will enable you to maximize the skill taught in Chapter 5. Furthermore, assuming that you haven't already learned it and want to learn it, doing that will enable you to learn another related skill and how to interpret it that is extremely useful in with respect to your project of living better.

Unless you may want one-on-one help, the Appendix is optional.

Just the fact that you're reading this demonstrates that you're willing to take charge of your own degree of emotional well-being (rather than remaining a passive prisoner of unwanted emotions and blaming other people or events for your distressing predicament). Once you accept that responsibility, it's just a matter of learning how to free yourself and then doing it. This manual will teach you how to free yourself. Then just do it.

I strongly encourage you to use the skills presented here. If you don't, the quality of your emotional life won't improve, your purchasing it will have been a waste of money, and your reading it will be a waste of time. If you do, you'll improve the quality of your life for the rest of your life.

Emotions are important. Emotional well-being is important. Flourishing emotionally is a critical part of living well. [See my Introduction to Living Well.]

Because you accept responsibility for the quality of your life, there's no reason or obstacle standing between you and a lastingly improved quality of life. More fulfillment is yours to claim.

I wish you well.   20 Apr 21

Dennis E. Bradford

Contents

1:

Introduction – Freedom and Truth

When we're in pain or dissatisfied, we yearn for something to heal us. The idea that the truth can do that is Biblical: "[T]ruth will make you free" [Holy Bible, John 8:32, Lamsa translation].

To be ignorant is not to know the truth. It's to be deluded. Truth is freedom from falsehood. Truth is reality. Truth and delusion are inversely proportional: the more truth, the less delusion, and the more delusion, the less truth.

Ignorance is curable; it need not be a lasting or permanent condition. How is it possible to tell that we are deluded and need to cure our ignorance? That's easy: *the more unhappy we are, the more deluded and less free we are.*

Are you as happy as you'd like to be? If so, this manual isn't for you. There's no reason for you to read any farther. If you aren't lying to yourself about that, if you aren't in bad faith with yourself about that, you're doing fine. Keep doing whatever you're doing.

Would you like to be happier? If so, this manual is for you. Why?

The idea of happiness correlates with the ideas of freedom and truth. The more you experience freedom and truth, the happier you are. The more you experience bondage and delusion, the unhappier you are. If you use the training in this manual, you'll diminish emotional bondage and automatically begin to enjoy more emotional freedom and well-being. **Happiness is a by-product of becoming freer and less ignorant**.

If you aren't yet as happy as you'd like to be and become happier, that will not only benefit you but those around you. Like it or not, your life automatically teaches others. It cannot not teach those around you. You are already an influencer. The only question is whether your influence is helping or hurting those around you. If you begin to enjoy more freedom from unwanted emotions, that will automatically benefit others as well.

This is an important point because of the counterproductive claim that we should not try to be happier because doing so is selfish. If you are not yet as happy as you'd like to be, you'd be wise to work on yourself to become happier. An important reason why is that that will benefit those around you, too. In other words, it's not selfish to be as happy as possible.

In truth, it's loving to be as happy as possible. The happier we are, the more loving we are. [See my Love and Respect.] Haven't you noticed that unhappy people are poor lovers?

Your purpose in life is to fulfill your potential and to become as happy as possible. [See my Are You Living Without Purpose?] If you disagree, it's probably because you have an incorrect or confused notion of happiness. Since the words 'happy' and 'happiness' are used in multiple ways, that's not really surprising. The justification for my position should become clear in what follows.

If your idea of happiness goes with the ideas of freedom and truth, you're zeroing in correctly on how to live better. If it also includes the ideas of being loving, peaceful, and joyful, your idea is dead on.

Don't worry: this manual offers training in three practical skills (techniques, methods). Although it includes some important contextual discussion about them, it's not primarily a theoretical account of happiness or its associated ideas.

Those ideas are, though, worth mentioning in order to put the three initial techniques in context and explain clearly why they are so useful. (The other two techniques concern helping others.) If you understand more clearly why these techniques work, you'll be able to use them more confidently and, so, use them better.

The concept of happiness I'm suggesting will become clearer in what follows. It's really a specification of the vague ordinary concept of happiness.

Assuming that you'd like to become happier, what's the plan offered here?

Do you realize that it's possible to measure (calibrate, calculate) happiness? Until the last year or so, I didn't. It turns out that a way to do that has been available for about a quarter of a century. The concept of happiness will become clearer when you learn how to measure happiness.

Since it's easier to improve what can be measured than what cannot be measured, the procedure for measuring happiness is an extremely important one.

Furthermore, if you become skilled at calibrating different levels of happiness, you'll realize that it's not only an invaluable tool for making decisions, but it can also be done quickly and easily in the privacy of your own home. Although it's not original with me, I'm delighted be able to pass along to you in this manual my understanding of it. I recommend that you test its usefulness for yourself.

Here's a relevant analogy. If you're trying to lose body fat, it can help to put a photo of your fat body on the refrigerator as a reminder not to overeat. Some fat loss experts recommend taking a sequence of snapshots to inspire you to do better as you are literally able to see your progress in slimming down. When you notice how far you've come by looking back at your successful progress, your motivation to continue will be strengthened.

A happiness calibration is similar. Just as nobody is forever stuck at a certain percentage of body fat, so nobody is stuck at a particular level of happiness. Just as we can gain or lose body fat, so we can raise or lower our happiness calibration.

Don't confuse your body weight with your percentage of body fat. If you lost ten pounds of fat and gained ten pounds of muscle, your body weight would be the same, but your percentage of body fat would have decreased and you'd be healthier. Using a scale at home, it's easy to measure body weight. Unfortunately, it's much less easy to measure body fat. The best way to do it routinely at home is to use plastic calipers once a week. If you then post the weekly calibrations from using the calipers on your refrigerator, you'll easily be able to track your progress or lack of progress with respect to decreasing your percentage of body fat.

Happiness calibrations are similar. They do, though, typically change very little over the course of a lifetime. If, though, you work on yourself regularly and effectively [See my <u>Emotional Empowerment: Killing Emotions</u> as well as what follows], you'll not only be able to avoid lower calibrations as you age but also you'll be able to record higher calibrations, and sometimes dramatically higher calibrations. **You may not only become happier, but much happier!**

After explaining what that means concretely and how to measure it, I explain in Chapter 5 the best way to undermine any unwanted emotion. That's the most important of the techniques presented in this manual.

Once you master that skill, you may naturally become so enthusiastic about it that you'll want to teach it to your interested friends and family. I explain in Chapter 6 how to do that well, in other words, effectively and efficiently.

Why, though, limit your teaching it? Why not help more people? I explain in Chapter 7 how to do that well and in a mutually beneficial way.

The first technique is the most important. If you don't at least use the technique presented in Chapter 5 to increase your own happiness, the time you spend reading this manual and any money you spent on it will have been wasted. Unless you are already flourishing emotionally, that would be a shame. Furthermore, the best way to help others solve a problem is to solve it first for yourself and then explain and demonstrate how you solved it. In that sense, sharing the techniques depends upon your successfully mastering your emotions.

Also available to you in this manual are two additional skills that, if you learn and use them, will enable you to maximize the value of the critical skill taught in Chapter

5. How to do muscle testing is explained in Chapters 2 and 3 and how best to use the results of muscle testing is explained in Chapter 4. The next chapter explains muscle testing and how to do it. Why? It's the skill required to measure happiness.

If you're serious about flourishing emotionally for the rest of your life, focus on Chapters 2 through 5. If you also want to help others do better emotionally after you've learned the critical skill in Chapter 5, focus on Chapters 6 and 7.

I encourage you to master all 5 skills. If you do, you won't regret it.

2:

Muscle Testing

If all you want to do is to learn how to dissolve any unwanted emotion, please skip to Chapter 5. *If you want to feel better for the rest of your life, mastering that technique is infinitely valuable.* Presumably, your wanting to learn it is why you purchased this manual. If that's your sole interest, that's the only chapter required. However, once you master it yourself, if you want you may share it with friends (Chapter 6) or with people who are not already your friends (Chapter 7).

Additionally, there's another skill that you may also decide to master that can be used to elevate the quality of the rest of your life, namely, muscle testing. The explanation for how to do it is in this chapter. Tips for improving your accuracy using it follow in Chapter 3. The method of understanding how to get the most value from learning how to do muscle testing is offered in Chapter 4. You may not only come away from reading Chapter 4 with a clarified understanding of happiness, but, if you get good at muscle testing, you'll also be able to understand how to measure not only your own degree of happiness, which makes it easier to increase, but also that of others. As is my policy, I'm trying to overdeliver.

Still, if you're troubled by prolonged emotional distress, if you are right now suffering emotionally, since that's very distracting as well as unpleasant, I recommend that you master the technique presented in Chapter 5 before reading everything else.

It's also a good idea not to underestimate the power of holistic healing. According to the National Center for Complementary and Integrative Health, there are a number of different kinds of therapies designed to balance or to bring energy into a patient's body. Some treatments involve light, sound, or magnets. Others such as reiki or therapeutic touch influence the energy fields that are in and surround one's body. Many physicians trained in western medicine now often consider these kinds of treatments as complementary to western treatments.

In fact, it's wise never to underestimate the power of a trained mind. For example, Dr. David R. Hawkins used his extraordinarily elevated energy or consciousness level to undergo two major surgeries without any anesthetic.

Here's one popular way to think of it: when our nervous systems and brains are working properly, we're bombarded daily with millions of bits of information or data from our environments that we must process just to continue to live. We are consciously aware of only some of that information. It all affects us physically, but only some of it registers mentally.

What happens to all the information that we absorb but are not conscious of? Does it just disappear? What if it's still there? What if we're able to access it physically? What if we extensively used such an ability as a truth or falsehood detector?

This is exactly what muscle testing may enable us to do.

Furthermore, it's not just for sages. I assume that, like me, you are not (yet!) a sage. I am able to make great use of it and there's no reason why you cannot do the same.

Our ability to accept a falsehood as a truth is why we're able to be deceived. Of course, acting on the basis of false beliefs can be extremely foolish and get us injured or killed. Strangely, though, many people are satisfied with their beliefs even when those beliefs may be false. In fact, many people are strongly attached to their beliefs and would rather live lives of poor quality than to detach from them. Why? One reason may be that it gives them an excuse for living poorly, which is a foolish, unsatisfying way to live. It makes living well impossible by ensuring that life cannot get significantly better. (This will make more sense after you read Chapter 4.)

Everything real has a vibratory energy field; every ordinary *form* (object, thing) radiates a specific, minute vibrational frequency, a tiny energy field. **Ultimately, every form is energy.**

For example, everything we do, say, or think produces an energy field. Even every thought, belief, attitude, emotion, or mood we experience radiates energy that can be detected. Every rock, tree, lake, mountain, or cloud has an energy calibration. Every animal, plant, virus, fungus, bacterium, or clump of plasma has energy that can be measured. Even every chunk of space has a minute frequency.

How can we apprehend that energy? When, for example, I look at a tree, I don't detect its energy field. So why even suppose that it has one?

The problem with such everyday examples is that *our perceivings are contaminated by our understandings and expectations*. In other words, what we perceive as adults is filtered through our conceptual systems. (It's not like that for a newborn baby. [I've discussed this in <u>Mastery in 7 Steps</u>.]) We normally never perceive what is real; instead, we perceive what we think is real. Perceivings are not neutral apprehensions. We perceive what we are conditioned to expect to perceive.

Concepts are principles of classification. If you're able to distinguish blue bodies from those that aren't blue, you have the concept of blue. Someone who is blind lacks that concept. Notice that, although someone born blind will lack such color concepts and, so, be ignorant of colors, that doesn't mean that colors don't exist. It just means that, because there's a failure of apprehension, that person is ignorant of colors.

If you live an examined life, as all philosophers try to do and all fanatics never even try to do, you already try to avoid impaired conceptual understanding. You deliberately try to keep learning, to keep improving your understanding. Since the everyday world is constantly in flux, we either keep up with the relentless becoming or fall behind.

Concepts are static. They deaden perception. It's easy to think of a lepidopterist who is so thoroughly absorbed with his classifications that he is able to look at a butterfly and fail even to notice or care whether it's living or dead. [I've discussed this in <u>Mastery in 7 Steps</u>.]

The domain of space and time, the world of ceaseless becoming that is the ordinary world we inhabit, is in perpetual flux. We deaden it when we conceptualize it. Since written words are immortal, the more literate we are, the more we deaden our daily experience of life. [See Abram's <u>The Spell of the Sensuous</u>.] This is so well understood by philosophers and psychologists that it would not be useful here to belabor the point.

The good news is that *consciousness (awareness, attentiveness) does not require thinking (conceptualizing, judging)*. For example, it's logically impossible for perceptual judgments (such as "that wall is blue") not to include what we may think of as partial thoughts that are mere noticings or singling outs of forms (such as the referent of "that wall") without judgments (labelings, predications, conceptualizations) about those forms. Logically, it's the difference between "x" and "x is F". You yourself may have used meditation or psychoactive drugs in order to relieve yourself temporarily of the heavy burden of the usual thoughts and worries we carry around. The fact that we human beings are able to free ourselves at least occasionally from the prison of thought addiction demonstrates that thinking is not the only way of being conscious.

Our ability to think is an important blessing. It's necessary for survival. It's sometimes critical to be able to distinguish friend from not-friend, food from not-food, and so on. Our ability to think is superior to that of any other animal species and, for better or worse, has enabled us to dominate the earth.

Always, one must pay the price. In this case the price is that, in a sense, we're too good at it. We get stuck thinking. The stream of consciousness becomes nothing but a stream of judgments. Our conceptual filters work so well that we get stuck living life in our heads rather than in our lives. This deadens our experiences and makes the world seem stale, repetitive, boring, and heavy. Playfulness evaporates.

Fortunately, there's a way to bypass incessant judging. It's possible simply to drop or detach from continual "thoughting." It normally requires a lot of the right kind of meditative practicing to do it, but it's not only possible but simple. Since waking up from everyday conscious awareness to what is sometimes called "superconsciousness" is possible, that demonstrates that we are able to apprehend directly and nonconceptually. It's analogous to waking up from dreaming to everyday conscious awareness.

If you yourself have not awakened in that sense, you'll naturally be skeptical that such a possibility exists. It's alright to be questioning, but please be kind to yourself and the rest of us and don't fall into the negativity of believing that it isn't real. Similarly, it's natural for someone born blind to be skeptical of colors, but that doesn't mean that colors aren't real.

This reminds me of the time I took a course in <u>tai chi</u>. During the first, 2-hour class the instructor kept talking about <u>chi</u>, but I had no idea what he was talking about. He told us not to worry about thinking about it, but just to practice the movements he taught daily. Guess what? To my surprise, after practicing the movements daily for only about a week, I began to feel the <u>chi</u>! I had simply never done what was required to open to it before.

Another analogy is to the practice of aliveness awareness, which I have described how to do in videos as well as in multiple writings such as <u>Emotional Empowerment: Killing Emotions</u>. All the cells in our bodies are alive and that aliveness feels good. The reason that we don't often feel it is because continual thinking absorbs all our attention. When we practice dropping incessant judging in favor of paying attention to the aliveness, our experiences of life become unbound from thought and we're able to experience the aliveness.

I hope that you've had similar experiences. The takeaway? Don't underestimate the power of your body. Just because you're able to think does not mean that you should always be doing it. Avoid the mistake of identifying with your thoughts. You are much more than just that.

Your body is the product of millions of years of evolution. It's programmed to survive and reproduce, which is why it is self-healing.

We learn about bodies objectively by perceiving them; we learn about bodies subjectively by experiencing them directly. The popular idea that learning about bodies "externally" is more important than learning about bodies "internally" is false. Why? It's simple: *perceiving is a subjective process.* Therefore, objective interpretations depend upon subjective experiences and not-vice versa. [For an excellent discussion of this, see Hawkins's I: Reality and Subjectivity.] In that sense, the rational depends upon the irrational. For example, you may use a bathroom scale to get an objective measurement of the weight of your body, but notice that your reading the scale is and must be a subjective experience.

Muscle testing is a well-known and frequently practiced technique for bypassing ordinary, incessant judging. It's a way of distinguishing true judgments from false ones that relies on the body as a way of getting around everyday consciousness. It's been around for decades, perhaps centuries. It's used widely by many holistic health practitioners.

There's a critical distinction in epistemology (the study of apprehension) between knowing and believing. *Beliefs* are thoughts that we attach to because we take them to be true. Beliefs can be true or false, but there's no such thing as false knowledge. For example, because (2 + 3) = 5 and crimson is a red, you cannot know that (2+3) = 6 or that crimson is a yellow. To *know* something is to find mistake in apprehending it impossible. [See Panayot Butchvarov's The Concept of Knowledge.] By way of contrast, it's possible to have many false beliefs. If it weren't, we could never change our minds or discover mistaken beliefs.

If so, then the really important epistemological problem is not about knowledge; instead, it's about belief. *How can we distinguish true beliefs from false ones?* The problem occurs because there may sometimes be no phenomenal or intrinsic difference between a false judgment and a corresponding true one. For example, in a dream you may become fearful because you falsely believe that a murderous fanatic is about to attack you.

Muscle testing is the best solution we have to that problem. Muscle testing is applied kinesiology. As understood by Dr. George Goodheart and Dr. John Diamond, it became an important clinical tool. In Chapter 4 you'll learn how it was further developed by Dr. David R. Hawkins to be of even greater usefulness.

I mention this because, if this manual is your first exposure to muscle testing and your attitude is a rational, scientific one, you're likely to regard muscle testing, like energy healing, as too woo-woo for you. Careful! That'd be just another common mistake of fanatically locking yourself inside your own conceptual prison. If you don't let go of it, you'll never free yourself. You'll never learn anything. Since, again, to limit your freedom is to limit your happiness, that would be sad. It's unnecessary. Therefore, I strongly recommend that, even if your initial reaction is that it's a lot of hooey, you nevertheless set your prejudices aside and test it for yourself. If you do, I predict you'll be very pleasantly surprised.

Learn from my mistake. I became a master thinker. I'm an intellectual who has read and written many books. In a sense, I maximized a natural ability I had. Apparently, I was born with an extremely high verbal intelligence and I used that ability to earn a doctorate in philosophy and then do productive work teaching and counseling undergraduates for 32 years. To enjoy success like that is not the same as mastering life. The truth is that for most of my life I was stuck in rationality.

There's nothing wrong with reason unless that's all one relies on to navigate life. Reason is extremely useful in undermining egocentric emotionality and, so, the conflicts bred by it. That's all to the good. In my case, until an important loss that affected me very deeply emotionally forced me to grow beyond rationality, the truth is that I was stuck without fully realizing it. When we stay stuck, when we stop growing, life not only loses its vitality, freshness, and playfulness but also by closing down we obstruct the possibility of living well, mastering life.

So, my suggestion is that you *learn how to do muscle testing*. Determine for yourself whether it is what it's claimed to be, namely, an important tool for improving the quality of our lives. Furthermore, if you're going to trouble yourself to learn it at all, learn it well. Why stop short of making it a tool that you're able to use regularly, even daily?

Since it's such a well-known technique, it shouldn't surprise you that there are lots of YouTube videos on how to do it. Of course, some are better than others. Furthermore, there are multiple ways of doing muscle testing.

If you have access to YouTube videos and it's still there, here's the one that I used to teach myself how to do muscle testing. I simply use the sway test. I do muscle testing myself, which eliminates the need to rely on anyone else. The instructional video is by Denice Davis. I suggest watching it more than once. After you've at least tested it for yourself, I also suggest watching other videos on the same topic to pick up additional tips from the experiences of others. After all, if we didn't learn from others, we'd still be living in caves. There's no point to insisting on making all the mistakes yourself, which is a dangerous and inefficient way to learn. Simply go to YouTube and do a search for "Denice Davis Kinesiology."

Hers is not a concentrated, focused video. It's long and chatty. Much of what she talks about is irrelevant to learning how to do muscle testing. However, she also demonstrates how to use it, for example, to tell the difference between supplements and foods that are a vibrational match for you and those that aren't. (You may find that that helpful tip alone is worth many times the price you paid for this book. Muscle testing everything that you ingest could save you decades of ill health. If it did, how much would that be worth financially to you?)

Muscle testing does have limitations. Three are most important. *First*, its accuracy is relative to the person using it, and some people are, at least temporarily, unable to use it. *Second*, it cannot be used to determine the truth or falsity of thoughts (propositions, judgments, statements) about the future. Why? The future doesn't exist and, so, has no vibrational frequency. Muscle testing is limited, therefore, to judgments about the present and the past. *Third*, its usefulness is limited to only precise statements that can either be affirmed or denied. These limitations will become clearer in what follows.

There's no one best way to use muscle testing. I recommend learning the simple sway test first and then, if you want, master either doing it using both hands or using one hand. I also recommend that you learn how to do it by yourself so that you don't always require someone else to do it. That said, here are the steps to use.

First, when it comes to doing it rather than learning about it, what's critical is to have a clear mind.

With respect to testing the truth value of some thought, ensure that you're not biased and prematurely attached to either a positive or negative outcome. Instead of a self-serving attitude unduly influenced by your favorite beliefs, muscle testing won't work for you until you *adopt an impartial, nonattached attitude* about seeking truth. Get your ego out of the way; detach from self-centeredness. The mind is more powerful than the body and, so, it can unduly influence the body. The purpose of muscle testing is to get the body rather than the mind to determine truth or falsity, so not getting the mind out of the way automatically undermines the accuracy of muscle testing calibrations.

Second, assuming that you're using the sway test, cross all your body's meridians to *ensure balance*. Ms. Davis demonstrates that in the video.

Here's how to do it. While standing up, cross your ankles. Then put your arms straight out in front of you and cross your wrists. Interlace your fingers and tuck your arms down and then pull your hands up in front of your chest. Drop your head down. Hold that for a few seconds.

Meridians are energy lines in the body that run just below the surface of the skin. Although they're not used in western allopathic medicine, they're used in eastern holistic healing techniques as acupuncture. If you don't ensure that you're rebalanced, you may get a false reading; you may get either a positive or yes reading that actually means "no" or a negative or no reading that actually means "yes."

Energy doesn't disappear. This is important to understand. As Ms. Davis recommends, it's helpful to think of your body as an energy library that you are reading by using energy testing, which is like a library card that gives you access. If you're unbalanced, the books you check out will be the wrong books.

Third, stand up and *do a thymic thump*. There are multiple ways to do this.

Ms. Davis teaches one way in the video: tap with the fingers of one hand in a circular, counterclockwise motion over the thymus for a minute or so. Alternatively, you may, with a closed fist, thump 3 times over your upper breastbone while smiling and saying 'ha-ha-ha' with each thump while mentally picturing someone you love.

You may use smudging spray as part of preparing to do muscle testing, but that's optional.

Fourth, *test* using a simple procedure to ensure that the technique is working properly. Test both positively and negatively.

It's simple just to use your name to determine if you get a positive response and some other name to determine if you get a negative response. For example, suppose I'm using the sway test. I stand still, upright but relaxed, with my arms at my sides, my feet relatively close together, and my eyes closed. I test "My name is Dennis" and "My name is Joyce." The former thought should be positive and the latter one should be negative. Notice that both are clear statements about the present.

A negative response is a momentary muscular weakness. Falsehood weakens the body. A positive response fails to exhibit a momentary muscular weakness.

Using the sway test, a positive response will make you fall forward and a negative response will make you fall backward. Often, it's rather strong as if, positively, someone had pushed slightly on your back to propel you forward, and, negatively, someone had pushed slightly on your chest to propel you backward. Sometimes, though, it's weaker and you'll stand upright for a moment or two before gently falling forward or backward and having to move a foot to catch yourself.

Fifth, structure the proposition that verbalizes the judgment that's to be tested clearly and precisely. *Ensure that the thought to be tested is stated clearly and precisely.*

While it's true that all sentences are corrigible with respect to their linguistic propriety, make the sentence about the subject proposition you want to test about the present or the past as clear and unambiguous as possible. Don't be satisfied with making it so that it can be understood; instead, try to make it so that it cannot be misunderstood. The best way to do that is simply to test alternative synonymous sentences both positively and negatively. Testing related alternatives is actually easy and quick to do. You can also test the same thought at different times or have someone else check it as well.

It's not just ambiguity that can be a problem, it's also the level of one's understanding or consciousness that's relevant. I explain this more thoroughly in Chapter 4. It's important because inaccurate calibrations can result not only from a poorly formulated yes-or-no statement but also from a too-low personal calibration of the person doing the test.

What's a "personal calibration?" I explain what that means in Chapter 4. Understanding it requires an understanding of a logarithmic scale from 1 to 1000 that was developed by Dr. Hawkins. Anyone who has a current personal calibration lower than 200 on that scale cannot get reliable results using muscle testing.

However, and this is important, since it's extremely unlikely that anyone reading this manual will have a personal calibration that low, don't now worry about it. Simply assume that your personal calibration is sufficiently high.

The accuracy of muscle testing results increases with the personal calibration of the person doing the muscle testing. Therefore, it would be a mistake simply to assume that each of your results is accurate. That would be assuming that yours is the highest possible calibration, which is extremely unlikely. Instead, assume that your results are probably reliable but not infallible. This is why it's wise to test any proposition whose truth or falsity is important to you using several different statements about the subject matter.

Like other kinds of measurements, muscle testing measurements have degrees of accuracy. The higher your personal calibration is over 200 on Dr. Hawkins's 1000-point scale, the more accurate your measurements will be. Until you become experienced using muscle testing and your personal calibration is at least over 500 (and preferably over 600), realize that there's always room for some error. For context, since 96% of adult humans calibrate at 499 or lower, you probably do as well. Therefore, you'd be wise not to bet your house on any single measurement.

Rest assured that the odds that your current personal calibration is between 200 and 499 are extremely high. If so and yet you keep getting inconsistent results, something else is going wrong. Since lots of energy healers have had that problem, there are lots of videos on YouTube that discuss how to improve your muscle testing technique. I offer in the next chapter tips for increasing your accuracy and also explain how to check the accuracy of your results. With sufficient practice and feedback, your results will become more reliable and you'll gain confidence in your ability. Once you've mastered the technique, muscle testing is not only fast and easy, but you can do it without anyone else knowing that you're doing it.

Sixth, *do it*. Once your preparation is complete by finishing the first five steps, clearly focus *only* on the statement or proposition [P] you want to test. Since what we understand is recontextualized each time there's a major paradigm shift in our ability to understand, I recommend that you relate P not only to that level of understanding but also to the 1000-point scale and say (out loud or silently to yourself) something like:

In the name of the highest good, on a log energy scale of human consciousness from 1 to 1000 where '200'

indicates empowerment and '600' indicates sagehood, P is true at 100.

If you fall forward indicating that it's true at 100, move up to 200, 300, and so on. When you get a negative response, if you want to get a finer calibration, simply back down to a lower number and start going up again until you get another negative response and then the previous calibration is correct. You'll quickly be able to zero in on a single-digit calibration if you want.

For example, suppose that I want to calibrate Aria's current personal calibration. I'd test to determine if her personal calibration was 100 or higher. Let's imagine that it is. Then I'd test to determine if it was 200 or higher. If so, then I'd test to determine if it was 300 or higher. If so, then I'd test to determine whether it was 400 or higher. If so, then I'd test to determine if it was 500 or higher. If it wasn't, then I'd drop back down to determine if it was 450 or higher. If it was, then I'd determine if it was 460 or higher. If not, I'd drop back down to 455. Then 456. Then 457. If it was true at 456 and not at

457, then I'd have determined her current personal calibration is 456.

This may seem tedious when written out, but in practice it's not. Once you are focused in on P, just repeat the *P is true at* ____ last part of the initial statement. Since *each test requires only a moment*, zeroing in on P's calibration actually only takes a few seconds. If you're just doing one test, you'll quickly realize that it takes longer to prepare to do the test using steps 1 through 5 than actually to do the test.

As you master muscle testing, your intuition about reading the personal calibrations of others will improve. In the example, if I know Aria and 456 is an unsurprising calibration, I'm done. If it surprises me, I could simply rerun the calibration at different times to determine how consistent the measurements are or ask someone else to run it also. (It'll become clear in Chapter 4 why having an accurate idea of the calibrations of others around you is important.)

As with most skills, there's a learning curve. You must practice it at least for an hour or two even to begin to get good at it. My recommendation? Practice it for just 10 minutes daily for a week or two. My prediction is that you'll not only find it easy to do with practice but also that you'll find its results interesting and frequently quite helpful.

How do you know if your calibrations are accurate? How can you improve their accuracy? The answers follow in the next chapter.

Also, what do those numbers mean? The answers are in Chapter 4.

Don't fret. Muscle testing is a critical tool for enhancing emotional freedom in the easiest way possible. You'll be rewarded with a great "aha" moment when you suddenly get the connection among the ideas presented in this manual.

3:

Improving Accuracy

Inconsistent results from muscle testing mean that the accuracy of your energy testing is poor. What should you do if you're getting inconsistent results?

If the inconsistency is small, in single digits, there's usually no need to worry about it. For example, if I test Aria's personal calibration on Wednesday and it's 456 and it's 457 or 458 the following day, that's too small an inconsistency to bother correcting. Actually, because personal calibrations may change over time, it may not be an inconsistency at all. Even if it is an inconsistency, it may just be due to a minor measurement error.

How much deviation is too much? That depends upon why you are doing the muscle testing. If it's just a couple of points but those are on different sides of a major shift [I explain in the next chapter what that means.], then you might want to be concerned. On the other hand, if it's 10 or 20 points within the same level, you may decide not to bother to be concerned and that's the more common occurrence.

It turns out that *the factors that influence accuracy are ones that also influence your happiness level*, the quality of your life. That's interesting, isn't it?

The first step in muscle testing that was explained in the previous chapter is to clear the mind. **Clearing the mind is the most important factor with respect to both muscle testing and living well.**

Living well requires making and sustaining a wholehearted commitment to truth. This is living an examined life, which involves frequent questioning. We all have biases and blind spots. We all have difficulty apprehending truth. We all suffer at least occasionally from believing what is false. Simply admitting this is important. Not admitting it is fanaticism. The more fanatical someone is, the more hellish that person's life is.

After fully admitting to yourself that you may have false beliefs, decide to do better about that. Decide to become more serious about living well. Do you think that basing decisions on false beliefs is a good way to make good decisions? Of course not.

You are not your thoughts. Step back from them and take a hard look at them. Of course, whenever you notice a prejudice, delete it. Detach from it. Just because it's a thought doesn't mean that it's true. For example, I've even known philosophers who, while ignorant of it, were biased against the whole eastern philosophic tradition! That's just foolish. Having a mind open to truth (reality, what-is) is the sine qua non of living wisely. Sages are never fanatics. The higher the personal calibration of a sage, the less fanatical that sage is.

The most important mental obstacle to using muscle testing more accurately is being close-minded, thinking that biases, prejudices, blind spots and possibly false beliefs are acceptable when they're not. The more fanatically you attach to your beliefs, the more likely it is that you'll never be able to use muscle testing accurately. [I provide a specific example of this in the first chapter of <u>Emotional Empowerment: Killing Emotions</u>.] Beliefs are always perspectival, relative to one's level of consciousness.

An attitude of clinical or objective detachment is required. Set aside *all* your favorite thoughts, beliefs, positionalities, and attitudes. Readmit them only if they withstand examination. [Essentially, this was the procedure recommended by Descartes in his famous <u>Meditations on First Philosophy</u>. 'First philosophy' refers to logically first philosophy, which is ontology, which is the study of reality (being, truth), and epistemology, which is the study of how we apprehend reality.] That includes setting aside cynicism and negativity. Since it protects us from premature attachment, it's good initially to be skeptical or questioning. However, the ideas that there is no truth or that there is no way to apprehend truth obstruct living well. [See Plato's <u>Meno</u>, <u>Gorgias</u>, and

<u>Theaetetus</u> as well as Hawkins's books for more about this.]

Thought has no mechanism that internally corrects it. This is a serious problem because, by distorting contexts, any foolish or immoral behavior can be rationalized and supposedly justified. Being a muscle tester should be like being a healer who adopts an attitude of detached objectivity in order to align with the truth.

Since this is seldom easy, really focus on the first step each time before you do any muscle testing. Suppose, for example, that you're worried about having an as-yet-undiagnosed illness. You decide to test a proposition like "I have cancer" or "I am diabetic." Naturally enough you hope that neither statement is true. However, our expectations are extremely powerful. Again, **our minds are more powerful than our bodies**, which is why our thoughts can affect the outcomes of muscle tests. So, it's critical to clear your mind, delete all extraneous thoughts, before doing any muscle testing.

In a case like this, you should want to know the truth about your health. Why? If you learn that you have an undiagnosed health problem, you may be able to take steps to cure or at least improve it or, minimally, take steps to prevent it becoming worse. If you're unaware of it, though, awareness of it may come too late to do much about it.

This is an example of why it's important to be detached from your own beliefs and open to the truth before you do any muscle testing. If you aren't, you'll undercut the reliability of muscle testing before you even begin. Adopting an attitude of detached objectivity about your beliefs automatically undermines any emotional biases you may have with respect to the outcomes of muscle testing. [I explain why in <u>Emotional Empowerment: Killing Emotions</u> and in other places.]

Since the purpose of meditation is to detach from thoughts (and, so, from all the beliefs and the emotions spawned by them), the optimal time of day to do muscle testing is after meditation. [I explain in multiple videos and writings the two meditative practices that I use, namely, aliveness awareness and zazen. For example, I teach how to do aliveness awareness in <u>Emotional Empowerment: Killing Emotions</u> and zazen in <u>The Meditative Approach to Philosophy</u>. I also demonstrate zazen in a YouTube video at <u>https://www.youtube.com/watch?v=k-MPaKA5oHiI</u> or find it by doing a YouTube search for "Kneeling Meditation" or "Kneeling Meditation Bradford".]

What's our most powerful ability? It's our ability to focus our attention. We're able to choose what to notice and attend to. This improves our ability to function. The ability to select a focal point and concentrate on it can be immensely strengthened by many different meditative (yogic, spiritual) practices.

Again, always, though, one must pay the price. The price for improving our ability is that "focusing is accomplished by excluding the whole" [Hawkins's <u>The Eye of the I</u>]. Intellectual vision may be conceived as centered (Yang) or peripheral (Yin). While

DENNIS E. BRADFORD, PH.D.

a classic meditative practice improves concentration, when practiced sufficiently what
happens in the paradigm shift at 600 is
awakening (enlightenment, realization) in
which all subject/object dualistic thought
dissolves. The apparent difference between
subject and object disappears. It's as if the
subject (the ego/I, the person) drops away.
This spiritual waking up is said to be the
greatest human experience and, since it
cannot be conceptualized, it cannot be described except negatively. For example,
unlike the rest of us, the lives of sages are
not attached to personhood or personality.
What that's like cannot be learned in the
usual way; it must be directly experienced.

If you are not now practicing properly
daily and begin, that will not only improve
the accuracy of your muscle tests but also it
will improve the quality of your life. There's
no one meditative practice that works best
for everyone. If you don't have one and want
to begin, I recommend starting with aliveness awareness. Whichever one you select,
I believe, as the Buddha taught, that it's

impossible to live well without meditation. The more successful you are at meditation, the more successful you'll be at muscle testing. Once you're in the right state of mind and calm, here are some additional tips for improving the accuracy of your muscle tests.

Ensure that you're well hydrated. If there's any doubt, drink a glass of water.

Really relax by simply taking several deep breaths and releasing them before you do a muscle test. When you inhale the air in, imagine that it is going all the way into your body and right down to your fingers and toes (even though you understand that it's not going past your lungs).

Shake your hands out for a few seconds while imagining energy entering from the top of your head and flowing into your body. Imagine that shaking out your hands is releasing it and that the rest of it is being released down your legs and through your feet into the earth. In other words, imagine your body as being energized by the universe.

Some people like to use Lavender & Sage Smudge Spray or some similar aura spray to spritz away negative energy. Except for your wallet, it can't hurt. You can spray it on your hands, above your head, or in your immediate vicinity. There are also smudge candles available.

Here's a final suggestion for improving accuracy after learning muscle testing, are following all the suggestions above, and are still getting inconsistent results: check the balance between the right and left sides of your head (brain).

There are different ways to do it. The following assumes that you have learned one-handed muscle testing. (If you haven't, you may easily find YouTube videos that teach how to do it.) Stand (or sit) upright as usual. Put the hand you're not using for muscle testing about an inch or so away from one ear and have your fingers and palm flat. Using the other hand, test the truth of "this side is strong" (at your personal calibration level over 200). Then move the hand you're not using for muscle testing to the other side of your head and test again. If both sides are strong, you're good to go. If rebalancing is required, rebalance and test again to ensure balance.

Some experts claim that 1 in 20 people have a balky autonomic nervous system that prevents relaxation and inhibits the left and right sides of the brain from communicating as well as they should. That could explain why, if you are, you're still getting inconsistent results.

If you suspect that you have that problem, Lifeware Y-Age Aeon patches are available for purchase that supposedly correct that problem. You wear them for a week or two on your body, mostly on various places on your head. The patches are expensive, about $80 for 30. I've not tried them, but if you think you have a problem and can afford them, they might be worth trying.

There's one final caveat. In his 1995 book Power Vs. Force, Dr. Hawkins admitted that about 10% of the population is unable to use muscle testing. He didn't know why. I'm not sure whether he ever revised that opinion before he died.

What if you've tried everything and you're still unable to get consistent results using muscle testing? Don't despair. Here's how to utilize its power even if you're unable to use it yourself. Just work around it. How?

Find a willing, trusted friend (to whom you are not married) and, if necessary, have that person learn how to do muscle testing well. Recruit your friend to do the testing for you, including using you as a subject. Of course, it'd be a good idea to do something valuable for that friend in return.

Now that you understand how to do muscle testing, how to increase the consistency of its results if you find them inconsistent, and even how to work around an inability to use muscle testing yourself, let's understand the basics of the theory concerning how to maximize its results.

4:

Measuring Happiness

If you've learned how to do muscle testing and you're getting consistent results, this chapter is optional. If all you want to do is to learn how to dissolve any unwanted emotion, skip ahead to the next chapter.

However, I do not recommend doing that. The reason is that you'll almost certainly miss some major benefits of being able to do muscle testing if you do. *If you're going to trouble yourself to master muscle testing, why not maximize its benefits?*

Furthermore, the next chapter will teach you how to dissolve unwanted emotions, which is maximizing its emotional benefits. You may do that without having a clue with respect to why it works. Why does it work? I briefly explain why in this chapter (and recommend reading resources for additional explanations if you want them). That explanation will also clarify the idea of happiness.

(Incidentally, muscle testing itself calibrates at 600, which is the level at which sagehood begins, on the 1000-point Map developed by Dr. Hawkins. It's not an accident, for example, that the workbook for <u>A Course in Miracles</u>, which I also recommend, is also 600. An important danger of having a personal calibration of 599 or lower is being too skeptical about such aids to living better.)

Our brains and hearts are about 73% water, which of course conducts electricity and has its own energy. All the perceptions, observations, and reflections we have are relative to our bodies. Human beings have the widest range of possible calibrations of all animal species; at every moment each of us has a personal calibration that can be mapped from 1 to 1000. During life, these calibrations are not fixed.

The effects of our personal calibrations are both physical and nonphysical. The most important non-physical effects are those related to your personal calibration, in other words, to your degree of happiness, and to those around you, in other words, to your interpersonal relationships.

You're not only probably ignorant of your own personal calibration but also, like the rest of us, you're also susceptible to influences from your environment. Since an important part of that environment is the people around you, if you want to live better it's important to know their personal calibrations as well as your own. Why? If you deliberately surround yourself mostly with people whose personal calibrations are as high as or higher than your own, you'll automatically be reducing the influence on you of those people with lower calibrations and increasing the influence on you of those people with higher calibrations.

The happiness level of someone else cannot be directly measured. Instead, it can be indirectly measured by measuring the energy level of that person's state of consciousness, which is what a personal calibration is.

Again, those calibrations correlate with reported degrees of happiness. [Hawkins and his students tested these tens of thousands of times.]

The higher your personal calibration, the happier you'll be. Why? It's because the less delusion you'll suffer from and the more freedom and love you'll enjoy.

An effective way to become happier is to associate with those who are as happy or happier than you and to avoid associating with those who are unhappier than you. [See my The 5 Secrets to Making Fast Changes for Good!] If you calibrate the personal calibrations of the 5 people you spend the most time with and those measurements all turn out to be lower than your own, don't be surprised if yours diminishes over time. If you calibrate the personal calibrations of those 5 and they are all turn out to be higher than your own, don't be surprised if yours increases over time.

Success leaves clues. For example, if you play chess and want to improve your game, should you regularly play inferior chess players or superior chess players? Play superior ones because you'll learn more by playing them than by playing inferior chess players. We learn more from our failures than from our successes. For example, if you want to get stronger, should you regularly hang around with those who are stronger than you or with those who are weaker than you? You should hang around with those who are stronger than you because you'll naturally begin to absorb their training habits.

Many unhappy adults look and smell good from the outside. They can look happy externally and yet actually be unhappy. That's why it can be difficult to determine another's level of happiness. Muscle testing solves that problem. When you use it to measure another's personal calibration, it won't be fooled by appearances.

Please notice that people often may have an influence on you even if you don't know them personally. For example, they may write the books, magazines, and blog posts you read. They may create the podcasts and music you listen to. They create the roads, buildings, and cities that surround you. If you want to live better, take more control of your environment. For example, if you want to read a book, if you know how to do muscle testing and how to use Hawkins's Map, before investing any money in buying it or any time in reading it you can determine its calibration as well as that of its author. Why not only read books that calibrate at 500 (or, even better, 600) or higher? Why not only read books from authors whose personal calibrations are 500 (or, even better, 600) or higher?

Similarly, it's impossible to live well without living. More people in human history have died from war than from any other cause including pestilence, starvation, and natural disasters [from Hawkins's Truth Vs Falsehood]. If you have the option of moving, why not use muscle testing to determine the best place to live at least in terms of its history, culture, dominant religion, and institutions? At least you could improve the odds by eliminating those countries or societies that rank below 300 or at least 200. Warning: if you research them using muscle testing, you may be in for some surprises!

With respect to your own personal calibration, you'll be able to increase it more easily if you're able to keep measuring it occasionally. Almost without exception in human history, everyone could have a higher calibration. What does that mean? Again, raising one's personal calibration reduces ignorance and increases freedom. What's the cash value of doing that? It increases the amount of love in our lives; we become better able to love and better able to receive and experience love. [See my Love and Respect.] It also increased the amount of abiding joy and peacefulness we experience. If you'd like those infinitely valuable benefits, raise your personal calibration as much as possible.

How much? That's the kind of question that benefits from the developments in muscle testing made by Dr. David R. Hawkins. For example, anyone with a calibration of 200 or higher on his Map of Consciousness has some ability to love. The further above 200 your personal calibration, the more love. He recommends that everyone aim for a personal calibration of 500 or higher because that's the level at which love really intensifies and blossoms. If you want even more, aim for a level of 540 or higher because that's the level of unconditional love.

It's critical to realize that personal calibrations merely reflect energy levels at specific times. For example, Adolf Hitler's personal calibration dropped from 430 to 40, which is the level of reptiles like Komodo dragons. For example, since 1994 by practicing spiritually I've raised my personal calibration 145 points to well above 540 (though still below 600).

Not surprisingly, *the chief way to raise your personal calibration is to emulate those who have done it*. Their chief tool is almost always some kind of effective meditative (yogic, spiritual) practice to purify the mind. Purifying the mind is emptying it of all thoughts and, so, also all the beliefs and emotions that come from them.

The chief way to stay stuck or drop your personal calibration is <u>not</u> to adopt a daily meditative practice.

The takeaway? If you want to be happier, practice some classic meditation daily.

One's social, cultural, and economic environment matters. For example, the average adult in North America calibrates in the low 400's while the average adult in the Middle East calibrates in the high 100's. This does *not* mean that the moral value of North Americans is higher than that of Middle Easterners. All human beings are equally valuable. An Adolf Hitler is no less *essentially* valuable than a Mother Theresa. However, they differ very widely in their personal calibrations and degrees of happiness. Of course, they differ immensely in the moral quality of their actions; one is a paradigm of what it means to be a good person and the other is a paradigm of what it means to be a bad person. The takeaway? If you want to be happier, exercise more control over your environment.

DENNIS E. BRADFORD, PH.D.

Here's the good news: "Spiritual endeavor and intention change the brain function and the body's physiology . . ." [Dr. Hawkins's Transcending the Levels of Consciousness] in addition to increasing your degree of happiness. How happy do you want to be?

If your personal calibration is below 200 and you bizarrely prefer the stress hormones like adrenaline and unnecessary physical illness to the endorphins associated with peacefulness and improved immunity to physical illness, don't work on yourself. The predictable result will be a continued lower quality of life than is necessary. If you prefer a hellish life to a better or even heavenly one, don't work on yourself. On the other hand, if you would like more happiness and an improved quality of life, work on yourself daily. The more intensely you do that, the better you'll live.

You may object that you'd be better off working on others. You may think that it's better to try to work on others than to work on yourself. I used to wonder about that, but now I've realized that that's not true.

Working on yourself is the best way to work on others. Instead of lecturing or telling others what to do, you are demonstrating what to do, which is a more effective way of teaching.

Also, if it's true that we all share the same essence or whatness, that our moral value is the same, working on what appears to be yourself *is* actually working on what appear to be others. Even a solitary hermit living in a remote mountain hut working daily on himself is benefitting all others if he's successful in raising his own level of consciousness. Why? By doing that he's raising the general level of human consciousness, which benefits all humanity.

Here's a critically important insight into the nature of reality: *All forms are interconnected with all other forms.* Ultimately, again, all forms have the same essence or whatness, namely, energy [Being]. Whether we realize it or not, every form is in an energy field such that it interacts with every other form. There is no entity, no real form that is somehow totally isolated "outside" reality. This is as true of mental entities like thoughts and beliefs and images as it is of rocks and stars.

For our purpose, it's important to notice also that it's true of emotions. *All emotions have energy frequencies that can be detected using muscle testing.* Valued emotions such as joy, serenity, and bliss have higher calibrations than unwanted emotions such as shame, guilt, grief, anger, and fear. Think of unwanted emotions as temporary afflictions or agitations that are best dissolved as quickly as possible. **The lower an emotion's energy field calibration, the more harmful that emotion is.**

Therefore, ranking emotions in terms of their energy fields yields a scientific way of determining which emotions are the most harmful. If you use muscle testing to yield calibrations that can be plotted on Dr. Hawkins's Map, you'll know which ones it would be best to dissolve first. Dissolve the most harmful emotions first.

If you work on yourself, it's natural to wonder, "Am I making progress?" Combined with Dr. Hawkins's Map, muscle testing provides a solution to that problem.

He developed a logarithmic Map of delusion/freedom (degrees of happiness, levels of awareness) that ranges from 1 to 1000. Notice that it's not an arithmetical scale in which the differences between levels are equal. So, for example, there is a significant difference between, say, 450 and 451.

I don't claim that Hawkins's Map is perfect. It's not a perfect system (for example, it's somewhat confusing about emotions), but it's not only the best I've ever encountered but also my qualms about it are only minor theoretical ones. It's the most useful way of classifying a huge amount of material related to our ability to understand that I've ever encountered. I've found it extraordinarily helpful.

For example, consider the ideas of living in heaven or living in hell. Many people confuse immortal life with eternal life. The natural result of that confusion is that they think of heaven or hell as existing after death. However, the idea that humans have a life span is, as the Buddha taught and Jesus suggested, itself a confusion to be avoided. (Both the Buddha and Jesus have maximum calibrations at 1000.) It's actually part of the stunning idea that, ultimately, time itself is a delusion, but you need not accept that idea or wonder about it now. What is eternal is outside time, timeless; it's not something that occurs at all times. This doesn't mean that there's nothing valuable about the ideas of heaven and hell. Living a heavenly life is the paradigm of living well, whereas living a hellish life is the paradigm of living poorly. Hawkins's Map enables greater clarity and specificity: anyone with a personal calibration of 199 or lower is living a hellish life and anyone with a personal calibration of 600 or higher is living a heavenly life. For those living with personal calibrations between 200 and 599, the higher their calibrations the happier they are.

For example, consider the popular and traditional idea that we human beings have a dual nature. We're half material (physical, bodily, corporeal) and half immaterial (angelic, spiritual, incorporeal). Hawkins's Map enables greater clarity and specificity. Material life occurs from 1 to 499 and immaterial life occurs from 500 to 1000. Someone living with a personal calibration in the 500s is a loving person on the threshold of sagehood, which requires a calibration of 600 or higher. It's not infrequently been noticed that, since they seem to be in this world but not of it, there's an element of otherworldliness about sages, whereas those who live with calibrations below 200 live as savagely and egocentrically as predatory animals.

The most important division on the Map occurs at level 200. Levels of 1 to 199 are levels of falsehood; levels 500 to 1000 are levels of truth. Hawkins explains the Map in a trilogy of books, namely, <u>Power Vs. Force</u>, <u>The Eye of the I</u>, and <u>I</u>. This is an excuse for me to mention another value of correlating muscle testing with the specificity of Hawkins's Map, namely, it relates to improving our personal calibrations. Just reading a good book can improve our understandings and, so, our level of consciousness, sometimes by as much as 35 levels!

Since it's a form, every book has a calibration. For example, <u>Power Vs. Force</u> calibrates at 850, <u>The Eye of the I</u> calibrates at 950, and <u>I</u> calibrates at 999.8! Although it's impossible to hang around with Hawkins directly because he died in 2012, it's possible to hang around him indirectly by reading his books, listening to his audio courses, and watching his interviews. (If you do, you'll find he has a good sense of humor and, like all sages, a cheerful, open, loving attitude.)

If you don't initially want to read that trilogy but want to get off to a faster start than you would without reading any of his books, I recommend the you read his <u>Letting Go</u>. Another good general introduction to his thinking is <u>Reality, Spirituality, and Modern Man</u>. If you have a particular problem that concerns you such as stress, anxiety, depression, alcoholism, obesity, or cancer, I recommend his <u>Healing and Recovery</u>. If you're learning to master muscle testing and want a book to test your calibrations, see <u>Truth Vs. Falsehood.</u>

All apprehension of truth is relative to a certain perspective. It's always perspectival. Every judgment is a conceptualization and, so, necessarily limited in the sense that it's logically impossible for it to capture reality as a whole. Concepts do intellectual work by sorting or dividing. If there were a notion so wide that it would encompass everything, if there were a proposition so all-inclusive that it purported to capture everything, it couldn't help us improve our conceptual understandings because it would be unlimited and, so, suffer uselessness because it would be terminally vague. Every intelligible judgment is limited. Conceptual understanding depends upon using concepts to sort or classify. (Of course, non-conceptual understanding or direct apprehension cannot be explained conceptually or verbally.)

Even Hawkins's Map is limited. He suggests that there are calibrations much higher than 1000 but that they remain beyond the ability of the human nervous system to apprehend. Still, the Map is all we need to understand to understand happiness and help us become happier.

Anyone with a personal calibration of 600 or higher is happy. Anyone with a personal calibration between 500 and 599 is happy and on the doorstep of optimal happiness. That leaves about 96% of humans who calibrate at 499 or lower and would like to become happier. Since those who calibrate below 200 fail to take responsibility for the quality of their own lives, this manual is really intended for those who calibrate between 200 and 499 who want to live better.

Is it possible to get an approximate idea of your own personal calibration without first mastering muscle testing and correlating its outcomes with Hawkins's Map? Yes. Here's how.

The levels of the Map are aligned with energy fields that can be calibrated. In nonlinear dynamics, these fields are called "attractor fields." What Hawkins's calls "the Lower Mind" may be distinguished from "the Higher Mind" according to his <u>Transcending the Levels of Consciousness</u>. Any level below 200 is Lower and any level 200 or higher is Higher. (Some nonhuman animals calibrate above 200.)

For the Lower Mind, the attractor field related to animal survival calibrates at 155. Animal survival is all about self-interest, in other words, not just physical survival but also personal pleasure, emotions, and gains. This is the domain of living poorly. This is the domain of Hell.

For the Higher mind, the attractor field related to spiritual awareness calibrates at 275. So-called spiritual awareness becomes increasingly attuned to the value of other beings. This is why it correlates with love: to love is to promote what is best for the beloved (as opposed to trying to use another to promote what is best for oneself). This is the domain of life between Hell and Heaven (sagehood, 600 or higher).

The chief point here is that someone with a consciousness level of 155 lives in a radically different world or surreality than someone with a consciousness level of 275.

The transition from Lower Mind to Higher Mind occurs at level 200. Why? It's at level 200 that selfishness begins to transition into selflessness.

Fairness, consideration, honesty, and ethics begin to prevail at 200 (and above). It's the level where love first emerges. As Hawkins puts it in The Eye of the I: "The mind is contaminated by emotions . . ." *At level 200 freedom from emotional bondage begins.*

What about sages and emotions? Those whose personal calibrations are 600 or above do not think dualistically and, so, they do not experience emotions as we nonsages do. Since sages have achieved nonattachment from selfish egocentricity, they are not emotional in the sense that nonsages are.

The core of every emotion is a self-centered evaluative judgment. [See, for example, my Emotional Empowerment: Killing Emotions or Emotional Facelift.] **A decrease in selfishness or increase**

in selflessness always automatically yields an increase in emotional well-being. The ability to love grows automatically as attachment to egocentricity diminishes.

To help determine whether Lower Mind or Higher Mind is more like your surreality without muscle testing, you may do a self-evaluation by asking yourself the following questions and honestly comparing your answers to those of sages (saints, people who are wise) who are familiar to you. Of course, if you lie to yourself or have no familiarity at all with people who have mastered the art of living well, your answers will be useless.

- Is an interpersonal relationship about taking or giving?
- Is it more important to accumulate possessions or to grow?
- Is it better to be only ego- or self-directed or also to be other-directed?
- Is life all about competition or cooperation?

- Should I attack or should we try to avoid confrontations?
- Should I be ruled by egocentric desires or by rationally chosen values?
- Am I frequently upset or tense or am I typically calm and deliberate?
- Am I quick to condemn or to forgive?
- Am I selfish or considerate?
- Do I pretend never to be wrong or am I humble enough to admit fallibility?
- Am I a sexist or a humanist?
- Do I frequently lie and prevaricate or do I always attempt to be truthful?
- Is what I ultimately value my egoic self or the spiritual Self?

Once you have the answers, you should reliably be able to classify yourself as either having a predominantly Lower Mind or Higher Mind. (Again, it's quite likely that you have a Higher Mind.)

According to Hawkins, only 15% of those at level 155 rate themselves as happy, whereas 60% of those at 275 do. Notice that that's a whopping fourfold increase in the reported level of happiness! This is a specific example of the claim that *the higher your personal calibration, the happier you are.* 100% of sages are happy.

Furthermore, for Americans, 275 is well below the average personal calibration even though half of all Americans calibrate below 200.

Again, for each of us, our degree of apprehension is relative to our level of consciousness. For example, someone who calibrates at 250 will be unable to understand someone who calibrates at 450, and someone who calibrates at 450 will be unable to understand someone who calibrates at 750.

Fortunately, since our personal calibrations levels are not fixed, we can improve them. That's good news.

Every level of conceptualization below 600 is its own limitation. If you are not yet a sage, or at least above 500, I encourage you to do better.

Ordinary thought ceases at all levels 600 or above. Sages calibrate at a level that is higher than the ordinary subject/object method of understanding and, so, cannot be understood conceptually. Sages have been pointing this out for literally thousands of years.

Assuming that you are not (yet) a sage and take responsibility for the truth in your life, you calibrate between 200 and 600, probably in the 200's, 300's, or 400's. I personally don't know many people who calibrate at 500 or higher. Like beauty and (genuine, lasting) joy, love is really beyond form. Form becomes progressively less useful at level 500 and above.

If you currently calibrate at 499 or lower, you're not stuck there. Nobody is ever stuck.

Raising your personal calibration significantly need not be difficult. "The transitions from one state to a higher state are not difficult to make." [From Hawkins's Letting Go]. He himself went from a religious upbringing as a child, then to atheism, then to agnosticism, and then to waking up spiritually. Many sages go through a similar progression. Many also tell us that sagehood, which is our birthright, is not necessarily difficult.

Why does it *seem* difficult for many of us? It's because of our level of understanding. Especially if we have worked hard to attain a certain level of understanding, for example, a rational or scientific understanding in the 400's, we are reluctant to let go of it. Our understandings become recontextualized at each higher level and that requires letting go of our previous contexts. We are so familiar with them and comfortable in them that it usually takes an important loss or some similar event to shake us out of our psychological slumber. This explains why something that seems difficult today may seem easy tomorrow. If we don't continue to grow and stay stuck, life seems always to continue to try to teach us the same lesson until we master it and go on to the next lesson. Except at a personal calibration level of 1000, there's always a next lesson.

What's usually (though not always) required for a major paradigm shift is the deprogramming of your mind by mastering some effective meditative practice to experience it. It helps us detach from conceptual obstacles that have been obstructing progress. Again, it usually takes an important loss of, say, health, a relationship, prestige, or money to stimulate us even to begin to try something like an effective meditative practice that might alleviate our suffering. As you may know, that's the way it worked for Eckhart Tolle.

As many people have discovered for themselves, a great benefit of letting go of attachments is that doing so automatically increases emotional well-being. In other words, prolonged emotional distress always diminishes as a result of proper practicing. Proper practicing is really surrendering and that always dissolves egocentric emotionality. Surrendering all the programming is waking up spiritually. [See Hawkins's Letting Go and Taylor's Waking Up.]

Removing emotional obstructions can greatly assist you in doing that. If you increase your understanding by reading this book and actually following the technique presented in the next chapter, you may enjoy enhanced emotional well-being for the rest of your life. *Your personal calibration will improve as you become happier. How much in dollars would that be worth? It's priceless.* You also then have the option of deliberately teaching others how to do the same.

5:

How to Dissolve Any Emotion

A *thought* is a judgment or conceptualization. A *belief* is a thought that we attach to because we think it's true. Although all are limited, some beliefs are true, but some that we think are true are false and so sometimes we unintentionally wind up attaching to false beliefs. Believing what is false is not a harmless mistake; it can easily get us injured or killed.

A critical difference between a belief and an *emotion* is that an emotion always has a physical location in the body.

Mother Nature gave us emotions because they can be useful with respect to survival. They motivate action without our having to think about what to do.

We enjoy emotions like joy or happiness that literally feel good. These are valued (preferred, desired) emotions. We suffer when we feel emotions like fear or anger that literally feel bad. These are unwanted emotions.

An emotion is not its consequences. Sometimes, valued emotions can have deleterious effects such as when we're doing something that makes us happy but that simultaneously prevents us from doing what would be of more benefit. Sometimes, unwanted emotions can have good effects such as when we experience fear that stimulates us quickly to jump away from a dangerous snake as soon as we notice it without having to think about what to do. Therefore, in terms of their consequences, valued emotions are not always good and unwanted emotions are not always bad.

Let's set aside any consideration of what it's right or wrong to do when prompted by emotions to do something. Let's also set aside any further consideration of valued emotions. They feel good and usually cause little or no trouble to enjoy.

Let's focus here on how to respond to prolonged unwanted emotions.

The natural response is to get rid of them by trying either to prevent feeling them in the first place or by trying to minimize that unwanted feeling after they arise by, for example, distracting ourselves.

I've elsewhere [in other writings such as <u>Emotional Empowerment: Killing Emotions</u> and <u>Emotional Facelift</u>] explained why the ordinary tactics for dealing with unwanted emotions fail. For example, simply trying to ignore an unwanted emotion fails for the simple reason that we have to remain aware of what we want to ignore. For example, acting out or venting an unwanted emotion either perpetuates or strengthens it, which is the opposite of dissolving it, which is what we'd really like. So, venting, too, fails.

If your personal calibration is 599 or lower, let's consider the one method that will work for you. It's a simple, 5-step method (technique, skill) that anyone can master quickly.

Understand that peacefulness is a characteristic of happy people. The happier we are, the higher our personal calibrations are, the more peaceful (serene, tranquil) we are. The happier we are, the less deluded and freer we are. Therefore, it's important to understand that you don't have to gain anything to attain greater peace of mind. All you need to do is to remove the obstacles that are obstructing you from enjoying it. In that sense, although you may not realize it yet, *you already are what you need to be.*

There are five steps required to dissolve any unwanted emotion.

First, **decide** to feel better emotionally and to do whatever it takes. Take responsibility for the quality of your emotional life. Assume control. Admit that nobody and nothing else has any influence over your emotions except you. Unless you give away your power, nothing external has any emotional power over you. Everyone with a personal calibration over 200 tends to accept emotional responsibility.

If you haven't already done it, it's time for emotional maturity. It's natural for children to be out of control emotionally, but that's wholly unnecessary and counterproductive for adults. Relief from prolonged emotional distress is available. This method is one that anyone can master by following these five steps. Commit yourself to doing it and just do it.

Second, select (pick out, identify, single out) the unwanted emotion that's obstructing your natural emotional peacefulness.

Emotions are always related to some situation (state of affairs, event) or other that you take to be relevant to your life. Select the unwanted emotion that relates to that situation. For example, if you just learned of your mother's death and are experiencing grief, her death is the situation and that grief is the unwanted emotion. There's nothing you can do to change that situation, but you are, if you decide to be, in full control of your emotional response to it.

Thinking about that situation and feeling that emotion are uncomfortable and possibly very distressing. You may experience prolonged emotional distress from that grief. Not wanting to feel that way is why you may try to avoid it. You may habitually try avoidance as a tactic for dealing with unwanted emotions. If so, this second step is counterintuitive. Just selecting it for your attention is the opposite of trying to avoid it. You'd be wise to break the understandable and normal, though counterproductive, habit.

Let yourself experience the emotion. That's what happens when you attend to it. Don't worry: letting yourself feel it won't kill you. Dissolving it requires full awareness of something to dissolve and fully accepting it.

You may be in the bad habit of doing the exact opposite. In the past whenever you experienced an unwanted emotion such as grief, shame, fear, or anger, you may have tried to think it out of existence as soon as you noticed it. If so, you know from experience that that doesn't work. It's a natural tactic to try, but, since it doesn't work, if you keep trying it, you'll just keep getting the same result, namely, the unwanted emotion will continue to be felt indefinitely. Unwanted emotions can be troublesome for months, years, or even decades.

Changing tactics is the way to alleviate them. Although it's counterintuitive, just keep noticing it and accepting it. That's all that you have to do.

Notice how all emotions want attention. In that way, they are like crying babies. What should you do with a crying baby if you want it to stop crying? You could change the situation so that you don't hear its crying by, say, putting the baby in a basement closet. You could make the baby stop crying by, say, giving it some drug to knock it out. The mature way to handle that situation would be to give the baby your undivided attention. Pick it up, rock it in your arms, and speak or sing softly to it. I grew up frequently babysitting for younger siblings and, in my experience, that almost always works – and it almost always works quickly, too. That's only an analogy and, like all analogies, it's not an exact one. However, you may find it helpful.

The **third** step is simply to keep noticing it and accepting it after you've selected it rather than trying to distract yourself from noticing it or trying somehow to force it to go away.

Emotions are most frequently felt in the front of the body, in the throat, chest, or stomach. When an unwanted one is, it helps to put the tip of a forefinger on the center of its location. Whether that's possible or not, stay single-mindedly focused on the center of its intensity. Whatever it does, whether for example it moves or contracts or expands, stay out of thoughts about it and simply focus intently on its bodily location.

Fourth, be with it that way for a few minutes. This just extends the third step. If you're willing just to be with it lovingly for 5 or 10 minutes, you may be amazed at how quickly most emotions either dissipate completely in that time or at least greatly diminish in intensity.

Sometimes an unwanted emotion won't dissipate completely in a few minutes, but they always weaken in intensity if they are loved unconditionally. You should then go back later in the day or the following day and repeat the process. Simply do that for as long as it takes. It can take a long time for an unwanted emotion to dissipate completely – but, if you stay with the process, that will happen, usually quickly but occasionally slowly.

Christen Mickelsen as an adult had a lifelong fear of heights. He decided to free himself from that unwanted fear and began working on it every day in the manner just described. He did it every day for several months and, finally, he proved that that fear had dissipated completely because he was able to parachute out of an airplane without a problem. That's a very unusually long time for this process to work. However, it could be that you encounter a similar unwanted emotion. It happens occasionally. So? That's life. Just accept it and work this process for as long as it takes.

By the way, there's no correlation between how long it takes and how long you've had an emotion or how intense it is. Sometimes, a mild, merely annoying emotion can take a relatively long time to dissipate and sometimes an intense, lifelong, inhibiting emotion can dissipate the first time you try this technique on it in just a few minutes.

There's an important life lesson here: **thinking is resisting**. The more you think about the unwanted emotion and try to force it to go away or resist it, the more you'll perpetuate its existence. This is why it's impossible to think it out of existence. **What we resist always persists**. The corollary is that what we accept diminishes in importance. In other words, *wholehearted acceptance, unconditional love, works*.

Fifth, test or check to ensure that the unwanted emotion has completely dissipated. Don't be afraid that it might not have disappeared; instead, check it to see. There's nothing to fear because this process has already greatly diminished its intensity to the point where you are just checking to see if anything is left. If there is, do more loving on it. If not, you're done – and it will never return.

The way to check is simply to think about the situation that gave rise to the emotion in the first place and notice if you feel that unwanted emotion at all. To use the same example again, think of your mother's death. Is there any grief left about that important loss or have you reached the point of total acceptance? If even a little grief is left, work on it some more.

Peacefulness is a natural, neutral feeling. Sometimes at the end of the process you may feel joy or relief, but that's not necessary. If you feel happier, that's fine. If you don't, as long as the unwanted emotion has completely dissolved, that's also fine. You are now emotionally free from bondage to it.

In short, **prolonged emotional distress is optional**. Sometimes, intense unwanted emotions occur. That's normal and natural. If you accept what life gives you, there's no problem. If you try to force an unrealistic alternative, there will always be a problem. In that case, though, you are creating the problem and, so, you have the power to stop doing that. You now have the 5 steps to go through whenever you want to free yourself from any unwanted emotion.

Permit me to end this chapter by answering two questions. First, are there any problems with using this method and, if so, how should they be solved? Second, why does this work?

First, there's a general problem with respect to treating any unwanted emotion and it's this: it may be interrelated with other unwanted emotions and, so, hard to single out for treatment. For example, often they come in clusters or layers. If you understand this, you won't be surprised if you encounter it.

There's no one-size-fits-all solution. Just single out the most intense unwanted emotion and use the technique to dissolve it completely. Then go on to any related unwanted emotions and work on each individually to dissolve them completely. Be patient. This is an example of the idea that freedom isn't free, in other words, freedom must be earned. As you work on dissolving them, congratulate yourself on doing what's required to live better by living more freely.

Notice two important features of this technique. First, it doesn't require any deep background analysis. No psychoanalysis required. No expensive professionals need to be hired. Even if you cannot remember the situation that spawned an unwanted emotion, this technique can still be used to dissolve that emotion completely. Second, it's easy to learn. You can actually teach it to an attentive, interested adult or older child in a few minutes. [These two features are important in the following two chapters.]

In case it gives you more confidence in this technique before you try it, permit me to mention that it's not original. Other sages and their students have advocated it and I learned it from them. For example, Dr. Hawkins discusses its central idea [in Transcending the Levels of Consciousness] and his student Christen Mickelsen has popularized it. Both Eckhart Tolle and Thich Nhat Hanh have also promoted its central idea. [For short, free video introductions to their work, I have several videos on both Eckhart Tolle and Thich Nhat Hanh in the *Emotional Empowerm*ent playlist on the DENNIS BRADFORD PHD YouTube channel.]

Although I think this is the best method of dissolving unwanted emotions as easily as possible, it's not the only one. I explain another one, which is promoted by Byron Katie, in <u>Emotional Empowerment: Killing Emotions</u>. I mention that here because recognizing the fact that there are multiple methods that are able to undermine unwanted emotions may help you drop the thought that flourishing emotionally is impossible.

Emotional well-being is not only possible, but it's possible for you.

Second, this technique works for the same reason that meditation works. That's because it is a meditative technique!

What is the ultimate source of all unwanted emotions? Death and fear of death.

Sages have not failed to notice this. For example, we read in A Course in Miracles, "death . . . is the one idea which underlies all feelings" that are not feelings of supreme happiness [Lesson 167 in *Workbook for Students*]. Since sages, in other words, people whose personal calibrations are 600 or higher, lack all fear of death, they never experience unwanted emotions. (Why? As I mentioned, they are free from bondage to dualistic thinking and don't take themselves to be separate persons subject to annihilation. [What sense does that make? As I argue in section 6.3 of Mastery in 7 Steps, they identify with consciousness which is similar to other qualities in that it does not go in and out of existence. If so, if they are consciousness and consciousness cannot go out of existence, they cannot go out of existence either, in other words, they cannot die. If death is not an option, there's no reason to fear it.]) Dr. Hawkins also helpfully offers in multiple books an "and so" argument for the claim that all unwanted emotions come from the fear of death. Trace the implications of any fear and you'll trace them to the fear of death.

Once you have the confidence from mastering this technique, it's normal to be enthusiastic about it and want to share it with others. The final two chapters consider how to do that effectively and efficiently.

6:

Helping Friends

L ove is giving; it's not taking. To love another is to give of yourself in a way that benefits that other; it's not to use or try to use that other to benefit yourself. Therefore, the more you work on yourself to reduce your egocentricity (your self-centeredness, your selfishness), the more naturally loving you'll become. This is why sages are the greatest lovers. They are the least egocentric and most selfless of us.

Typically, too, they're the most cheerful and happiest people; they have, if any at all, the fewest grievances or complaints. They naturally attract others who want to be around them and enjoy their positive energy.

You now have a valuable gift to bestow on those of your friends who may be interested if you want to do so.

If you're interested in doing that, you'd be wise to avoid two mistakes.

First, avoid trying to teach anyone else the method before you have mastered it. Without experiencing how well the process works yourself, you will not have the confidence to teach it well. If others suspect that you don't really know what you're talking about, they won't listen to you about it anyway and that would damage your credibility. The process is always: *learn, do, teach*. Avoid jumping from learning to teaching without doing.

What should you do before you master the method if you encounter someone who is really open to learning it? Simple: refer that person to this book. If it's a friend and appropriate, you might even purchase it for your friend. Until you yourself are an expert who has mastered the technique, that's how you could still benefit someone else by enabling that person to learn from an expert.

Second, avoid trying to teach people who are uninterested. That's rather like, as the old saying has it, trying to teach a pig to sing – not only will you fail but you'll annoy the pig. Nonphilosophers are either not interested in living well or not serious about it. Although all nonsages want to do better emotionally, many don't want to talk about it or even use the method if you taught it to them anyway.

Strangely, people are often attached to their problems. (Why? I don't know. Perhaps they think their problems give them a good excuse for not living well. To my mind, that's foolish. Why not solve or dissolve problems to live better? Then again, though, I'm a philosopher.) Just be careful about annoying nonphilosophers. Never forget that they are usually fanatics who often really hate philosophers. Those kinds of people literally killed Socrates.

Friends are like family we've chosen ourselves. You didn't choose the family members you grew up with. Don't be surprised if none of them are philosophers.

It'd be a good idea to sit down with a cup of tea or coffee early some morning and write out by hand a list of your friends, acquaintances, and family members who might be interested in living better emotionally. Don't write down people who should be interested in living better emotionally; all nonsages should make that list. Only write down those who might, under favorable circumstances, actually be interested. When in doubt, though, write down someone's name.

That list won't be long. It probably won't have over 150 names and it almost certainly will have less than 100 names. At least try for 75 names. That's your initial list of prospects, people you'd like to help.

What do the people on that list think most about and like to talk most about? That's easy: themselves. So, the next time you encounter them (and you might want to arrange matters so that that happens sooner rather than later), get them talking about themselves. How? Ask questions about what they've been up to. Ask about such topics as their family, their work, their play, and their motivations.

I've never been a master at social interactions. Instead of being an extrovert who is energized by them, I'm an introvert who is exhausted by them. I've learned to use the acronym 'FORM' to help me with rapport-building small talk. The 4 letters stand for Family, Occupation, Relaxation, and Motivation (or Money). Asking a stranger about those topics with genuine interest (and using follow-up questions) has really made social interactions smoother for me and, I hope, more beneficial for others.

Remember that your friend already knows and likes you. If you didn't also know and like your friend, why would you be friends? It's easy to be concerned about the quality of life of someone you know and like.

It's no-good pretending to care about them. Actually care! Trying to fake love is being fraudulent. If genuinely caring about others doesn't come easily to you, this will make it easier: realize that we all share the same life. In other words, *essentially*, you are not different from your friend. Of course, nonessentially you are separate and different from your friend. The truth is, though, that what you and your friend are essentially is the same. In that sense, as Aristotle put it, a friend is another self.

Who controls a conversation, the person who talks the most or the person who asks the questions? Contrary to what many people believe, it's not the person who uses more words than anyone else; it's the person who leads the conversation by providing the topics under discussion. That's done by asking effective questions. So, do try to control the conversation by asking questions to focus the discussion on your friend's life and quality of life. Get your self out of the way. When you're tempted not to do that, remember that you have two ears and one mouth and interpret that to mean that you should listen at least twice as much as you talk.

The keys to mastering the art of conversation are to listen deeply and to ask good questions. To listen deeply is really to pay attention to what your friend says (rather than, say, formulating what you are going to say next when there's a break in the conversation). Paying attention requires being open-minded. Really focus on what your friend is trying to say without prematurely evaluating it. The truth is that, just by listening deeply, attentively, and nonjudgmentally to what your friend is saying, you're already blessing your friend. A surprising number of people are walking around with the feeling that nobody is listening to them, which can prompt the feeling that nobody really cares about them. The result is that they often feel unnoticed and unloved. Merely noticing what your friend is saying is already loving your friend. *Pay particular attention to the exact words and phrases* that your friend uses in describing his or her life and remember them. [The reason why is given below.]

If, sooner or later, your friend tells you about problems or grievances, resist any urge to give advice unless it's asked for. The truth is that we never know what to do.

(Why? Knowing is finding mistake inconceivable. Both actions and inactions have future consequences. These consequences are relevant to whether a decision is right or wrong. It's also true that these consequences are not only unknown but unknowable. So, our human condition is that as adults we're responsible for our decisions but we're unable ever to know what is right or wrong to do because we're always ignorant of what the future consequences may be. Presumably, you already understand this because you've had experience making important decisions and realizing that you were not in the position of knowing what to do. There is no knowledge of right and wrong.) Even if you could know what someone else should do about some situation, simply by stating it without being asked to state it you might unintentionally create resentment; your friend might interpret it as an implicit criticism.

As usual, the right attitude is humility. Accept the reality that you not only don't know what your friend should do, you don't know what you should do! Being humble promotes being empathetic. Try to understand your friend's life from inside it rather than from outside it. Usually, that's more interesting, too.

What should you do to ensure that your friend feels listened to? *Repeat in a summarized way out loud exactly what your friend has said using, insofar as possible, the exact same words and phrases that your friend used.* "Let me see if I understand you. You _____" To fill in that blank well, you'll really need to listen for and remember the exact language as your friend is initially describing his or her situation and remember them. If you really pay attention, your friend will undoubtedly get the feeling that he or she has really been listened to deeply.

That's important. Why? It's because *when your friend hears you describe that situation as well as or, preferably, even better than he or she has, then your friend will automatically begin to believe that you know what to do about it.* That's not necessarily true, but it's what will happen. That has the effect of opening your friend up to any suggestions from you. If you make suggestions that will benefit your friend, you've now strengthened your friendship by being a better friend.

Yes, it's a kind of trick. Your friend, though, is very unlikely to notice it. Make sure that you use it to benefit your friend. For example, use it to suggest that your friend learn the method presented in Chapter 5 and, if he or she does, you'll have benefitted your friend in a lasting way.

In general, what should you do if you think that you do know something that might help your friend? Instead of telling your friend your solution and assuming your friend doesn't already understand it, ask your friend questions <u>a la</u> Socrates that would lead your friend to apprehend the solution you recommend. Simply by asking questions, you may actually be of assistance that's really appreciated. The skill of Socratic questioning is a skill that you'll perfect over time if you practice it. Especially if you're able to pile agreement upon agreement, you'll have sold your friend on the value of your proposal. [See Neil Rackham's Spin Selling.]

Somewhere, reciprocity will kick in. Your friend will almost certainly sooner or later realize that he or she has been monopolizing the conversation by talking much more than you have. When that happens, you'll likely be asked how you've been doing. There's your opening. You've earned it!

In anticipation of that opening, create some succinct words that sound like something you'd normally say. Memorize them and practice saying them out loud word for word until they become natural. Then at that point say something like: *"You know how difficult it often is to shake a prolonged unwanted emotion like grief or shame? I recently learned how to solve that problem."* Opening with a question draws a listener in and using so few words about an important topic almost guarantees curiosity from your audience.

So, even if only to be polite, you'll likely be asked *"How?"* Since every nonsage wants to feel better, your friend will probably really be interested.

You respond, *"Would you like me to teach you? It's simple and would only take a few minutes."* If your friend isn't interested, that's not a problem. Finish that conversation as normal and go on to another friend. If your friend is interested but really doesn't have the time right then, immediately set another time to get together.

If your friend does have the time, say something like, *"Great. I'm now on a mission to help the world feel better!"* Say it in a fun way. Get your friend to agree in advance that, if the demonstration is successful, he or she will introduce you to 2 other people you don't know who probably don't know the method (because few people do) and who also might like to learn it. Not 1 other person and not 3 or more: exactly 2. If you don't get the references or agreement that they'll be provided after a successful demonstration, don't do the demonstration. Let your friend stew, which may only increase your friend's curiosity.

In other words, **make this a collaboration rather than a lecture**. You'll help your friend if your friend will help you to fulfill your mission.

If you do get agreement that the 2 references will be provided after a successful demonstration, excellent! Help your friend actually diminish or dissolve some unwanted emotion that he or she is now experiencing and would like to be free from. Do *not* attempt to explain the process as I did in the previous chapter. Instead, just help your friend through the process.

Decide. Select. Accept. Be. Test.

Your friend has already decided to try to dissolve the emotion, so that requires little or no coaching from you.

Your friend already has selected an emotion to dissolve so that also requires little or no coaching from you. Some people, though, for example many North American males, do have difficulty simply detecting and labeling emotions. That's sad and sometimes funny, too, as when some guy thinks he has a stomachache when it's really grief because his girlfriend dumped him the day before. If necessary in such cases, be empathetic and helpful. It's necessary to select and label one so that there's an emotion to dissolve.

Get your friend to accept feeling that unwanted emotion. It's not something irrational; it's just an emotion. How? If necessary, explain to your friend that it's part of his or her life and that not accepting it is simply fighting with himself or herself. One always loses such a fight. Accepting the emotion, even though it's unwanted, is just accepting a part of life that is already there. Accepting that it's there is just noticing reality instead of trying to be blind to it.

What may take 5 or 10 minutes is getting your friend just to be with it. If possible, use the tip of the forefinger technique. Explain the critical idea of loving it unconditionally instead of trying to force it to go away. Simply be encouraging. Have your friend, preferably with eyes closed to aid concentration and using the tip of the forefinger technique, just be with the most intense part of that emotion. Be encouraging. *"That's right."*

"That's it." "Just stay with it." "On a scale of 1 to 10, how powerful is it?" "There's no need to think anything – just follow it." "Good, just keep focusing right on the most intense part." When it begins to change or to move, say something like, *"Excellent. When it's moving, it's moving out."*

Ask after a silence, *"What's happening in your body now?" "Is it as intense as before?" "Has it begun to change yet?" "On a scale of 1 to 10, how powerful is it?"* Whatever the answers, *"Just stay with it. Keep focusing on it. No need to think – just be with it."*

Because you've mastered the technique yourself and perhaps even used these same or similar phrases while you were dissolving an unwanted emotion, you'll naturally communicate confidence in the process and be patient as your friend goes through it because you understand from experience how beneficial the outcome will be.

Almost certainly there'll be one of two outcomes. *First*, it will reduce in intensity. It may drop from a 9 or 10 to a 7. It may drop from an 8 to a 3. It may drop from a 6 to a

2. Whatever. That's success! All your friend has to do is to repeat the method again later or tomorrow and stay with it for more decreased intensity. If your friend does follow through, the complete dissolution of that emotion is assured. *Second*, it will have disappeared completely. If so, have your friend imagine the situation that spawned it and ask if anything at all is left. If so, your friend should repeat process until it dissolves completely. If not, you're done.

If it fails for whatever reason, you've not earned the references and don't ask for them. (I've never had that happen, but it's not unthinkable.)

At that point, you've blessed your friend twice. You've not only listened deeply, but you've also taught your friend a priceless method for living better emotionally forever.

Once he or she really practices and really understands the power of that method, you may get more than just 2 references!

Realize that it would be natural for your friend to want to reciprocate. One reason we sometimes refuse gifts or even just compliments is because we don't want to have to reciprocate. Of course, you already love your friend and would gladly help your friend to live better emotionally without any reciprocity.

However, realize that that might leave your friend wanting to reciprocate. So, even if you never use them, *getting references from your friend is good for your friend as well as potentially good for those other people as well as for you.* Making it a collaboration is better than making it a one-sided giveaway.

What should you do with those references? Follow up or not. It's your decision. I don't know what you should do, and I've explained earlier in this chapter why I don't know. Whenever we do something, it's a shot in the dark.

If you want to follow up and *if* you want to collaborate with people other than your friends about their emotional health, then the next chapter is for you.

7:

Helping Others

Unlike friends, the people that they refer you to do not already know and like you. Why does this matter?

People are more likely to buy from those they know, like, and trust than from others. This is why, for example, businesses spend so much effort and money on marketing or advertising. The more we encounter a business online or offline, the more aware of them we become. Attention is the coin of the realm. All things being equal, if you had to choose between A who you didn't know and B who you did know, who would you choose? Exactly.

The next factor is likeability. Especially if you enjoy being aware of some business's marketing, you'll tend to grow to like them. For example, every so often there are very clever and fun ads that are like mind viruses that stick. You yourself have some all-time favorite ads, don't you? This is also why many businesses spend so much effort on social media. If they can repeatedly entertain you, educate you, or, better, both ("edutainment"), you'll likely like them. If a business can get you to know and like them, all they have to do is to get you to trust them to make it more likely that you'll buy their product or service.

This typically requires multiple contacts, minimally seven. If someone is trying to get you to trust them, it's important that that person encourages you to keep reading blog posts, listening to podcasts, watching entertaining ads, or reading articles or books. Doing that time after time after time naturally builds trust. For example, if this is the first book of mine you've read, you'll likely trust me less than if it's the tenth book of mine you've read.

Once someone else knows, likes, and trusts you, that person is more likely to follow you and to become your customer, client, or patient.

The reason that you have a jump on others with respect to teaching the technique of dissolving unwanted emotions to strangers is because you have borrowed your friend's trust. Let's say that your friend Chris gave you a reference to Betty. Betty trusts Chris and, so, is already inclined to trust you simply because Christ trusts you enough to introduce you to her.

Be congruent. Be trustworthy. Do not betray Chris's trust. Genuinely try to befriend Betty.

How? Develop rapport. Except for Chris, you're strangers. Watch for commonalities. Ask questions with a genuine interest in her life. Find out her likes and dislikes. See if any overlap with yours that you can discuss and bond over. It need only take a few minutes.

Why? Here's how life works: *if you want something, give it away*. If you want a punch in the face, give one away. If you want a hug, give one away. If you want a friend, give friendship away; be a friend first in order to make a friend.

You're in communication with Betty to serve her, to love her, to give to her, to benefit her. You are not there to take from her. If possible, you're there to create a win/win outcome. Lead with the giving hand.

Be unfailingly polite, considerate, and courteous. For example, if you're talking on the phone, ask soon after connecting whether or not this is a good time for her. If so, fine – and she'll notice that you were considerate enough to ask, too. If not, simply reschedule.

Spend a few minutes establishing rapport. If you'd like to ask her a question, before you do that, ask her if it'd be alright for you to ask her a question. Tell her a little about yourself first and try to get her talking about herself. What's her educational background? What's her work? Is she a reader? What's the weather like where she is? What does she do for fun or vacations? What's her age group? Don't grill her; instead, just chat about ordinary things for a while. Especially notice any similarities that you can use to build on for ongoing rapport.

My father was a clinical internist who worked hard and scheduled patients every 15 minutes. He had a good sense of humor (probably from his Irish mother) and always seemed to have a new joke of the day. He once told me that one technique he employed to maintain rapport with patients was always to try to find one specific topic from their personal lives that was important to them to ask about during each visit – and he'd actually keep that written in the physical medical file he kept on each patient. For example, if he discovered that a patient enjoyed fishing, he'd always ask every visit about that. Although he himself wasn't an avid fisherman, he was an occasional fisherman and, so, that was a point of connection. It helped patients to relax and established a bond that naturally went beyond the physician/patient relationship. It cemented a person-to-person mutuality of interest.

Once you've established some initial rapport and received permission to ask questions, it's time for some version of the well-known Dan Sullivan question. *Ask it and* then shut up and *be completely silent* until Betty answers.

If we were having this discussion a year from now, looking back at your experience both personally and professionally during that time, what has to happen in your life to make you feel happy about your progress?

Even if the silence becomes uncomfortable, it's critical that you give her time to digest the question and answer it. Do <u>not</u> talk until she does.

Once she answers, do three things.

First, thank her for her honest answer. Assuming that you mean it, add that if you ever come across something that might help her, you'll pass it along – a magazine article, perhaps, or a URL to a related YouTube video. Following up is an important skill.

Second, relate her answer to freedom from obstructive, unwanted emotions. For example, suppose she replies that she's engaged to get married or that she'd like to get married. You might talk about how emotional neediness is a turn-off. Does she have any fear about getting married or having children? Issues like those are important, so tread lightly. That's sufficient to give you the idea. Since emotions are important, if she happens to mention anything that relates to interpersonal relationships, you should be home free.

Third, let her know that you yourself recently learned something relevant. Just as you did with your friend in the previous chapter, say something like "*You know how difficult it can be to dissolve unwanted emotions like fear? I recently learned how to do that.*" Pause and give her a chance to ask if she's interested enough to ask. If she does, proceed as in the previous chapter. If she doesn't express an interest, you might ask her if she might also like to learn it. More subtly, you could just plant the seed and end the conversation. "*Well, if you ever find yourself in a position where you're hurting emotionally and get back to me, I'm confident that I'll be able to help you help yourself."*

If she does express an interest, explain that it cost you time and money to learn, which is true if you paid for this book, read it, and practiced dissolving your own unwanted emotions. Also explain that she'll learn better if she has some skin in the game. She won't value the technique as much if she doesn't compensate you for teaching her. We all often evaluate a product or service in terms of how much it cost us. We tend not to value what we get for free. Try to get her agreement about that.

Help her, too, to imagine how much better her life will go if she lives knowing that she forevermore has the ability to dissolve any unwanted emotion. Emphasize the freedom value of the technique.

Then mention your usual fee. You'll have to test different fees to find which works best. Don't worry about it in advance; let the market determine it. No matter how high it is, some people will be able to afford it; no matter how low it is, some people will be unable to afford it.

One method to test is a price-drop. You could say, for example, *"My usual fee is $49, but, because you're a friend of Chris's, if you're willing to do it right now, I'm willing for you to cut that in half and I'll teach you how to master the technique for just $24.99."* Or use $29 and $14.99. Or $99 and $49.99. Test your local market to find out what works.

Be sure to take away her financial risk by adding something like, *"There's a 100% guarantee of a full, immediate refund if I don't help you either completely dissolve some unwanted emotion that you actually have right now or at least significantly dissolve its intensity – and you'll be the judge of whether that happens. I, too, am Chris's friend and I want you to be completely satisfied."*

If she's not at all interested, drop that topic and end the conversation naturally.

If she agrees, get her investment *before* teaching her the method. Assuming it works as usual, emphasize the priceless value of what she just learned and how little she invested to obtain it. Ask her if she happens to have 2 friends who also might be interested. End the conversation as you normally would. Of course, if it doesn't work, immediately refund her money completely with no hassle and then end the conversation as you normally would.

What if she says that she doesn't have that much money? Ask her to suggest an alternative amount. If she names one and you're agreeable, do it for the lower price.

If she really doesn't have enough money, try bartering. Does she have something of value that she could exchange for learning the method you'll teach her? Perhaps you can get a new shirt from a clothing shop she runs or a meal from a restaurant where she works. Try bartering with people you already know such as receiving a discount on your rent from your landlord or on service for your bicycle or automobile. We don't have to use money to make business deals work. There's never any tax on such exchanges either.

You may not have any desire to charge anything at all for your teaching. If so, that's alright; it's wholly up to you. Again, though, realize that charging something not only removes an obligation to reciprocate on the part of your student but will also give your student a stake in the outcome. In other words, charging something actually benefits your student as well as you.

If you have already mastered it, you know the value of the technique present in Chapter 5. Is it worth $1000? Is it worth $5000? Is it worth $100,000? Is it worth $1,000,000? That's your call, but I happen to think that learning how to flourish emotionally is priceless. In other words, except for charging so much that you never get any clients, you cannot charge too much for your teaching that technique others.

If you do make teaching this method a business, the key to success is to do it consistently. You'll not only get better at teaching as you practice teaching, but also contacting people will become habitual. Decide to do it for 5 or 6 days every week for the next 12 weeks. Commit yourself to doing the following: **contact 3 new people every working day** to determine if they might be interested in learning the method. Of course, if you want more success, make it 5 or 10. However, 3 is sufficient to build your business while ensuring that you don't burn out.

If you do make it a business, you'd be wise to check with an accountant and a tax attorney to ensure that you're following all applicable laws and statutes.

After your new business becomes successful and you become better at teaching, why not charge a higher price? Raising your price may not only put more money in your pocket, but it may also improve the desire to learn on the part of your students. Charging a higher price, though, requires psychological preparation on your part. If you haven't mastered the method yourself, you won't have the confidence to charge a higher price. If you have, you will. Obviously, the more clients you attract at a higher price, the more money you'll make. So, again, do yourself and others a favor and don't try to skip from learning to teaching. Before you even try to teach anyone else, master the method yourself.

What about muscle testing? If you want, you may also master that technique and charge for teaching it. Again, though, before even trying to teach anyone else, it's important to master it yourself. Also, since it can easily be learned for free from YouTube how-to videos, it'd probably be better not to charge anything for it and simply point them to those videos.

As far as maximizing the benefits of both muscle testing and the technique for dissolving unwanted emotions, to learn more about the theory behind them I wholeheartedly recommend reading Dr. Hawkins's books. It never ceases to amaze me how much wisdom there can be in a $20 book.

I hope that, after reading this manual, you have that same attitude about the technique for dissolving any unwanted emotion. If so and if you decide not to try to help others by teaching it yourself, why not bless your friends and others by recommending this book or, even possibly, giving it?

I welcome your feedback and wish you well.

About the Author

Dennis E. Bradford is a philosopher who holds a diploma from Blair Academy, a B.A. from Syracuse University, an M.A. from The University of Iowa, and a Ph.D. from The University of Iowa. Panayot Butchvarov, Distinguished Professor Emeritus of Philosophy at The University of Iowa, was his dissertation director.

Dr. Bradford has been a philosopher since 1964. He taught philosophy and humanities at SUNY Geneseo for 32 years. His duties included counseling students. He taught all the major philosophers from both the western and the eastern philosophical traditions.

Christian Mickelsen was his primary coaching mentor. Dr. Bradford only holds certification as a qualified personal coach from the Rapid Results Coaching Academy, but also he's undergone Instant Miracle

Mastery training and been certified as an Instant Miracle Master. In other words, he's also a qualified energy healer in addition to being a certified life coach.

He's a former member of MENSA and the American Philosophical Association.

He's the author of over 30 books, has been an Amazon Bestselling Author, and has an Amazon Author Central page. He's also published numerous articles, including 20 at https://ezinearticles.com/, as well as several hundred blog posts at his blog at dennis-bradford.com.

He's been a member of the Rochester Zen Center and became a formal student of its abbot, The Venerable Bodhin Kjolhede, Roshi, in 2000. Dr. Bradford has had a daily meditation practice since 1994. He volunteered for many years leading meditation groups for prisoners at both the Attica Correctional Facility and the Groveland Correctional Facility in upstate New York.

He spent 2 years as a lieutenant in the U.S. Army with overseas duty in Korea for 13 months prior to graduate school.

He played (full contact) hockey for many years in the Rochester Metro Hockey League. He regularly does both strength and fitness exercise.

He lives peacefully in his home on the shore of Conesus Lake in upstate New York.

Appendix:
Getting More Help

A re you familiar with the Hawthorne effect? It's a psychological effect that psychologists learned about from psychological stimulus/response studies. How do we react when we realize that we're being observed?

It turns out that we typically modify our behaviors in response to becoming aware that someone is watching us. Businesses and other organizations including governmental agencies make use of it frequently. Over time the power of the Hawthorne effect wears off, but nevertheless it can be quite useful.

For example, suppose that you've never exercised since you graduated high school and decide that the time has finally come.

A good way to proceed would be to hire a personal trainer who will watch you as you begin your exercise program. In addition to the guidance you should receive, an important reason why that will enhance your progress is simply because an interested party is watching you exercise.

If you cannot afford a personal trainer, although you'll have to learn yourself how to exercise, you could still take advantage of the Hawthorne effect by vividly imagining that a personal trainer you've hired is watching you exercise every session for at least the first month you train. If you do that, it may well stimulate you to practice more perfectly even though in this case the observer is imaginary.

Interestingly, our brains cannot easily tell the difference between what is real and what isn't. Reality is not a phenomenal quality such as being red or being circular. To be real is to be multiply singleoutable, the subject of multiple identity judgements [For more on this, see my The Concept of Existence or Butchvarov's Being Qua Being.] This is why we can be fooled into having emotional re-actions to what isn't real in dreams or men-tal illness. It's also why imagining someone watching you can stimulate you to improve your behavior.

Still, after a month, the power of the Haw-thorn effect may diminish and you wouldn't actually have anyone helping you.

If you were going to take up, say, golf or surfing, would you go it alone or would you hire an expert to ensure that you began properly? The latter is preferable because, otherwise, you may soon find yourself need-ing to unlearn bad habits, which is typically much more difficult than learning the right habits initially.

Mastering life is like that, too.

So many people are realizing the value of hiring an expert teacher that the online coaching industry right now is booming and rapidly growing.

Do you want to attract a mate? Do you want to become a better lover? Do you want to dissolve unwanted emotions that persist? Do you want to lose body fat? Do you want to launch your own business? Do you have a serious parenting problem? Hire a coach!

Because of the Hawthorne effect, simply hiring someone to watch you may by itself stimulate you to modify your behavior. Of course, having a coach who has expertise in whatever you are trying to do and with whom you quickly develop rapport is far superior to just hiring an observer. A good coach will not only "hold space" for you to develop but will also help guide your development. A good coach functions like a father figure, such as Virgil does for Dante in Dante's great <u>Comedy</u>.

Suppose that you want more peace of mind and more emotional empowerment. **What's the most important criterion you should look for with respect to hiring a coach?** Although the value of hiring a coach is relatively well-known, the answer to that critical question is not relatively well-known.

The most important criterion is the coach's degree of happiness. If your understood Chapter 4, you understand that someone's degree of reported happiness correlates directly with what can be measured, namely, that person's personal calibration (level of consciousness, degree of wakefulness, awakeness). While Dr. Hawkins's Map has been around for just over a quarter of a century, the idea behind it has been understood by sages for thousands of years. For example, the Buddha distinguished four different levels of awakening for sages.

The more conscious (awake, attentive, aware) someone is, the happier that person is and the more loving that person is. Someone's personal "awakeness" can be measured (calibrated, detected) by using muscle testing [See Chapters 2 and 4 above].

So, if you're thinking about hiring a coach, I recommend that you look not just at that coach's credentials or expertise in the area that interests you most but also at that coach's ability to love you, to support and encourage you to do what's best for you (in exchange, of course, for the money you invest in the coaching). Coaching is a collaboration, an exchange of value.

How, though, is it possible for anyone who is not an expert to recognize someone who is an expert? If you yourself are an expert, you don't need to hire an expert to help you help yourself. However, if you yourself are not an expert, you are liable to be conned.

This is a general problem concerning hiring anyone from a plumber to a personal coach. Assuming that you're not (yet!) a sage, how is it possible for you to recognize a sage who would be a loving coach? It's not. Sadly, there is no standard certification and there are con artists in every field.

If your personal goal is to become a sage, the good news that it is not initially necessary to find a sage to help you. However invaluable it might be, the personal help of a sage is not necessary in the beginning. (All the sages I've personally known began their quests by reading books or taking courses.)

Instead, all that you need to do is to find someone who has successfully solved your problem to help you to solve it, too. If that person has a track record of helping others do the same thing, so much the better.

Once you understand that your personal calibration correlates with your degree of happiness, it becomes obvious that **the way to become happier is to increase your personal calibration**. You might think about finding a sage to teach you. That's unlikely. There's one sage in fewer than ten million people, that's 1 in 10,000,000. Even if you found one, you'd likely have difficulty convincing that person to teach you individually.

Fortunately, it's much easier to find a personal coach to help you one-on-one. If you want that kind of help, the key is to find a qualified coach who has a sufficiently high personal calibration.

If you'd like to hire one and have some money to invest, the good news is that there are such coaches available to help you. How might you recognize one?

My recommendation is that you contact some to see if they'll buy you an initial coaching session. Start by doing browser searches or by looking at relevant groups in social media platforms. It not only is possible to do this without spending any money, but also, if a coach agrees to buy you an initial session, you'll be able at least to determine for yourself the initial degree of rapport between the two of you. If someone is a con artist in a field in which you're not an expert, that person will more easily be able to con you on the level of thoughts than on the level of emotions. That's why it's wise simply to have a conversation with that person and "listen" to your gut.

If your own personal calibration is sufficiently high and you've mastered muscle testing and understood how to interpret its results in according with Dr. Hawkins's Map, you could also or alternatively test that prospective coach's calibration yourself. Again, the higher your own personal calibration and the better you are at muscle testing, the more accurate that calibration is likely to be.

Unfortunately, if you happen to have a low personal calibration or have little or no experience muscle testing, you won't be able to do that. You may, though, be able to find or perhaps hire someone else who is qualified to calibrate a prospective coach for you.

[If you're stuck and would like to hire me for a modest, one-time fee to calibrate one or several prospective coaches for you, simply email me at dennis@endfearfast.com, tell me what you'd like me to do for me, and make an offer. If I happen to know a prospective coach's calibration already, I'll give it to you free. At the time of this writing, the only life coaches I know who have personal calibrations over 500 are me, a friend of mine, and Christian Mickelsen, but most other coaches I've not calibrated for myself. (Mickelsen is extremely expensive; currently it'd cost you six figures just for one day of coaching.) If you give me one or a few names and I accept your offer, I'll be able to provide you with my calibrations of them. Like most academics, most personal coaches calibrate in the 400s.]

If you're not acutely suffering emotionally, it's usually a good idea to straighten out your thinking by reading books and taking courses by those who have mastered the art of thinking. As an undergraduate I read some relevant books such as Philip Kapleau's <u>The Three Pillars of Zen</u> and Alan Watts's <u>This is It</u>. Although I found their ideas interesting, I never made use of them until I experienced an emotional crisis later in life. All the understanding required you already have available in this book.

Another frequently beneficial procedure that may not cost you a penny is to find a qualified spiritual teacher who regularly teaches groups and become a member of that group.

Still, *if you want fast results* find a qualified personal coach with whom you are quickly able to establish a connection that feels right to you and who is willing to work with you one-on-one at an investment you are able to afford.

If you happen to like that idea, let me offer an even more specific suggestion. Assuming I'm still doing them when you read this, because you've invested your time and money in this book and are still interested, *I'm willing to buy you an initial emotional assessment coaching session* with me to help you. It will include at no charge my own calibration of your current level of consciousness.

So, if you're interested in living better emotionally, using the Hawthorne effect well to your advantage, and in getting more guidance as well as personal support from me, I encourage you to schedule an initial telephone session with me. Since you're serious enough to have invested in this book, I'll buy the session for you.

Why might you find it helpful?

- You'll come away with a crystal-clear vision of what it would be like for you to end emotional confusion and distress and begin flourishing emotionally
- We'll uncover hidden challenges that may be sabotaging either your inner game or your outer game success
- You'll learn your own personal calibration, which will enable you to understand how far your evolution

needs to proceed until you experience to the next major paradigm shift of consciousness
- You'll leave the session renewed, re-energized, and inspired to do a lot better in terms of your emotional well-being and happiness

How would it work? These sessions typically last between 30 and 90 minutes, but you may want to allow for 2 hours. All that's required is a quiet place to be alone and undisturbed on the phone with me. Go to: https://calendly.com/dennis-47/session

Just answer the few simple required questions there and select a time that works well for you.

These calls are ends in themselves. The paying clients who invest in my Emotional Empowerment and other coaching packages enable me to be able to afford to give them away.

Our lives are not only terminal but short. By the time you read this, I may not be giving them away anymore. Sorry! (I'm in my 70's and may soon retire or die.) If you're interested, therefore, I recommend that you take immediate action and schedule one right now.

If I'm *not* making this offer anymore and you're acutely suffering emotionally, get some help promptly at least to help you get back to normal. Find a suitable consulting philosopher, psychiatrist, clinical psychologist, spiritual teacher, or friend willing and able to help you.

All the best!

www.ingramcontent.com/pod-product-compliance
Lightning Source LLC
Chambersburg PA
CBHW060257050426
42448CB00009B/1665